Every Word

Read Your Bible in 90 Days.

It's Not Extreme. It's Not a Challenge.

It's Basic Discipleship.

Joe Kohler

For the glory of God.

For from Him and through Him and to Him are all things. To Him be the glory forever. Amen.
–Romans 11:36

Table of Contents

Acknowledgements

I am thankful for the many opportunities I have had to study the Bible with groups and individuals over the past fifteen years. This has been one of the most fruitful activities I've been able to participate in. Anyone can read the Bible on their own. Studying the Bible in community requires a commitment from others, too. I'd like to thank, in general terms, everyone who has committed to the task and stuck with it until the end so we could grow together as brothers and sisters in Christ. The value gained from this has been, and I trust will always be, a tremendous blessing.

I'd also like to express my gratitude to my beloved wife, Beth. It is impossible to articulate the value of her constant, consistent, and godly contribution to our family, to me personally, and to our ministry.

A final thanks should be extended to my brother in Christ, Chris R., who read the entire manuscript and caught several typos. Any errors that remain are entirely my own.

Introduction

But He answered and said, "It is written, 'MAN SHALL NOT LIVE ON BREAD ALONE, BUT ON EVERY WORD THAT PROCEEDS OUT OF THE MOUTH OF GOD.'"
(Matthew 4:4)

I hear it all the time.

I need to get in shape.

People make resolutions to lose fat. Build muscle. Eat better. And so on. Improving your physical health is certainly worthwhile.

Scripture acknowledges the value of physical training and discipline. However, godliness is more beneficial.

> On the other hand, discipline yourself for the purpose of godliness; for bodily discipline is only of little profit, but godliness is profitable for all things, since it holds promise for the present life and also for the life to come.
> –1 Timothy 4:7–8

I don't hear people planning to discipline themselves for godliness nearly as often as I hear of people trying to get in shape. Do you?

Like your physical health, improving your spiritual health isn't something that can be done for you by someone else. You can buy all the right equipment, study the best methods, and understand the proper nutrition and recovery protocols. But if you don't apply the effort and do the work, you will gain nothing.

You don't make gains pushing play and then sitting on the couch watching other people exercise.

The author of Hebrews puts it this way:

> "All discipline for the moment seems not to be joyful, but sorrowful; yet to those who have been trained by it, afterwards it yields the peaceful fruit of righteousness."
>
> –Hebrews 12:11

If you want the peaceful fruit of righteousness, you must first be trained by the discipline of the Lord.

You need to put in the work. But nothing says that you need to do it alone. Pursuing goals in community is a beautiful and beneficial process.

Many people fail to improve their physical health because they don't see their plan through until the end. They give up too soon.

Others fail because they don't know what to do, how long it will take, or what to expect. When they hit an obstacle, they get frustrated. They quit before reaping the results.

Sometimes a personal trainer can help. Someone who has a plan. Who can provide realistic expectations and accurate timeframes for results to be seen. Someone who can encourage you along the way to not give up. To endure until the end.

That's what this book is for. It's a spiritual personal trainer. But it can't do it for you. You have to put in the time and do the work.

This is a blueprint for success. Follow the program. You will see results in 90 days. Guaranteed.

A person hiring a personal trainer isn't looking to earn a degree. They simply want someone to tell them what to do so they can reach their goals.

So, this isn't a scholarly book. If you want in-depth study materials, there are other resources for that. I have suggestions recommended on my website: www.fourthyearministries.com.

This book is intended to be just like a personal trainer. It tells you what to do today. One step at a time. If you put in the work, you will attain the goal. You will read your Bible, cover to cover, in 90 days. No need for before and after photos.

People commit to 90-day transformation programs with long workout sessions, cardio requirements, and rigid nutritional restraints. These programs, if followed, often leave people exhausted, sore, and cranky. All for results that are of some benefit.

The program in this book likewise requires commitment. It requires dedicated time and focus. But it won't make you sore. Instead of starving yourself, you will feast on God's Word. The results, if you're trained by it, will be the peaceful fruit of righteousness.

Are you ready to commit to developing your spiritual well-being over the next 90-days? Do you have what it takes to complete the course?

Be warned: this program might stretch you. It will likely ask you to read larger sections of Scripture than you are accustomed to. If you stick with it, the big picture will emerge. You'll make connections that you've never noticed before simply because you picked up the pace and didn't forget everything from the Old Testament by the time you got to the New.

It is possible to take a more aggressive approach. Feel free to do two-a-days, completing the program in 45-days, or even three-a-days and read the Bible cover to cover in one month. I don't recommend a slower pace, though.

The pace of the program, as outlined in this book, may seem intense. But it isn't extreme. People have become accustomed to spending *hours* indulging themselves. Yet, most think reading more than three chapters in Scripture at one time is fanatical.

This is nonsense. It's spiritual atrophy.

This isn't intended to be a one and done program. The hope is that you will build new habits that will continue for life. Your spiritual health is worth it.

So, put down your phone. Turn off the TV or whatever else may distract you from giving your best effort. Grab your Bible. Let's get started.

How To Use This Book

The plan is straightforward. It is simple. That doesn't mean it will be easy. The hardest part will be dedicating yourself. Putting in the work.

It is good to understand what to expect. The format of this book is intended to support you over the next 90 days as you feast on the Word of God.

The program contains four different types of sections. Here is a brief summary of each.

Warm Up

There isn't a *Warm Up* every day. These are found before main groups of books in the Bible. They give basic, helpful information for the reading to come. They are not exhaustive or deep. They are meant to get you ready for what is immediately ahead.

Day X

Each day has a section of Scripture to read. This is the heavy lifting. An attempt has been made to keep the sections similar in length. However, priority has been given to making sensible breaks that will be most beneficial for comprehension and retention. So, some readings are longer. Others are shorter. The average reader will need about an hour and a half per day. Just ninety minutes.

Most people have no problem dedicating such time to physical exercise and even *more* time to personal entertainment. It is more fruitful to dedicate this amount of time to Bible reading.

Form Check

Immediately following the daily reading is a section highlighting points of interest. This is <u>not</u> intended to be exhaustive. It doesn't cover every detail and nuance. It is intended to be read **after** the main reading is completed. These sections are here to reinforce the main reading. Like physical exercise, going through the motions is not the goal. We must check our form to be sure we are getting the most out of each exercise, both physical and spiritual.

Cool Down

After the reading of a book of the Bible is completed, there is a *Cool Down*. It is the counterpart to the *Warm Up*. These sections point out main theological themes. In some cases, they will also briefly address important related questions that are often asked when reading the Bible together in community.

Reflecting briefly on each *Cool Down* section will help the reader to retain the information and build upon it in the future.

Understanding the basic plan, all that remains is to get started. Are you ready? You can do it!

Before You Get Started

Equipment

Make sure you've got the proper equipment.

You're going to need a Bible. My recommendation is the New American Standard but any translation you have will work. Don't use a paraphrase.

You may also want a journal to take some notes along the way. You don't need anything special or fancy. A simple, inexpensive spiralbound notebook from your neighborhood dollar store will work great.

Some of what you read may be confusing. It may raise questions. Write it down. As you continue to read, you may gain new clarity. You may also want to note things you'd like to think more about or study in greater depth later on.

Supplements

You don't need any supplements for this 90-day program. The Bible is enough.

If you can get a Bible without any notes, that is your best option. If the notes aren't there, they can't distract you. If your Bible has notes and you don't want to buy a new one, then just discipline yourself to avoid reading them for the full 90 days. Don't worry. They'll still be there 91 days from now.

Mindset

A lot of people get bogged down by the names of people and places. Especially in the Old Testament. Don't let this trip you up.

You're not looking to become an expert at pronouncing them. If you get to something that is hard to pronounce, just do your best. Move forward.

As you read more, you will become more familiar and comfortable with some of these difficult names. Don't beat yourself up or let it bog you down. Just keep pressing on.

Commitment

There are going to be a lot of reasons to quit. Don't. Make the commitment. Let your yes be yes. Some days will be tough. Do it anyway.

Consistency, dedication, and discipline are required. Your investment in your spiritual growth is worth it. It's not going to be easy. But it will be worth it.

Let's do this.

The Program

Warm Up: The Pentateuch

Genesis, Exodus, Leviticus, Numbers, & Deuteronomy

The first five books of the Bible are often grouped together and called by different names.

- The Torah
- The Pentateuch
- The books of Moses
- The book of the Law

Each of these terms are used by some to refer to this collection of five books in the Bible.

Scholars debate who wrote these books. Scripture unanimously attributes them to one human author: Moses. If Moses wrote all of these books, then they were written between 1450—1406 BC.

We will assume Moses as the author of the Pentateuch for this program.

These five books form the foundation upon which the rest of the Bible is built. Properly understanding the content of these books cannot be overstated.

Day 1

Read Genesis 1–12

Form Check

Genesis 1—2 God is the sovereign Creator of all.

Genesis 2:4 In this verse, the word LORD appears in all capital letters for the first time. You will see it many more times. This is not the Hebrew word for Lord. It is the divine name: יהוה (YHHW).

Genesis 3 Rebellion and the curse. Sin and death. God promises to put to death the enmity (Genesis 3:15).

Genesis 5:24 Enoch is the first person characterized that he "walked with God." He won't be the last.

Genesis 6:9 Noah, too, walked with God.

Genesis 7 Judgment is brought upon the earth. Salvation is provided in and through the ark.

Genesis 9 God gave Noah a command and made a covenant with him.

Genesis 10:8–12 Babylon and Assyria will be important later on. Both were established by Nimrod.

Genesis 12:1–3 This covenantal promise to Abram is the foundation for salvation in both the Old and New Covenants. Remember it.

Day 2

Read Genesis 13–25

Form Check

Genesis 13:14–18 God makes a promise to Abram.

Genesis 15 This promise and covenant is the foundation of salvation by grace through faith.

Genesis 15:2 Look at the phrase "Lord GOD." The divine name (יהוה) again is printed in caps as GOD.

Genesis 16 Abram and Sarai foolishly and sinfully attempt to fulfill God's promise by their own means.

Genesis 17 Abraham is called to walk with God.

Genesis 18:19 The family unit is critical in protecting and propagating God's Word. This will remain a priority throughout the rest of Scripture.

Genesis 19:36–38 This shockingly records the birth of the fathers of the Moabites and Ammonites.

Genesis 21:1–8 God's promise is miraculously fulfilled. It was not a work of the flesh.

Genesis 22 Although God spared Abraham's son, He will not spare His own Son whom He will give as a sacrifice for the sin of the world.

Genesis 25:19–26 God's sovereignty is displayed in His choice of Jacob over Esau while in the womb.

Day 3

Read Genesis 26-38

Form Check

Genesis 26:2-5 God confirms His covenant and promise to Isaac.

Genesis 26:24 God will be faithful to do as He said because of His promise to Abraham.

Genesis 27:30-46 Jacob stole the birthright (Genesis 25:27-34) and blessing of his elder twin brother. Jacob's actions are sinful and unrighteous. God did not choose Jacob because he was worthy.

Genesis 34 This chapter records the actions of Simeon and Levi, Jacob's second and third-born sons. Jacob will pass over them when he blesses his sons at the end of his life.

Genesis 35:9-12 God's promise and covenant are reaffirmed. Jacob's name change is again declared.

Genesis 35:22 Reuben, Jacob's eldest son, commits a despicable deed. The blessing will pass over him.

Genesis 37 Joseph's dream is sovereignly given by God. It sets in motion events that will take place over many years. The imagery of this dream (Genesis 37:9-11) will appear again in Revelation 12:1. Like Jacob, we should keep this saying in mind.

Day 4
Read Genesis 39-50

Form Check

Genesis 39 God is working all things together for good, according to His purpose.

Genesis 41:50–52 Joseph saw his sons as a blessing from God in the midst of trouble and affliction.

Genesis 41:25–37, 53–57 God's sovereign purpose in the famine will be important for Exodus.

Genesis 46:8–27 Jacob's family goes to Egypt.

Genesis 47:20–26 Everything has proceeded according to God's sovereign plan.

Genesis 47:29–31 Joseph fulfills this request in Genesis 50:1–14.

Genesis 48:15 Abraham and Isaac walked with God. Israel urges Joseph's sons to do the same.

Genesis 49:8–12 The blessing to rule passes over Reuben, Simeon and Levi, and is given to Judah. The Messiah comes from Judah's lineage to fulfill this.

Genesis 50:22–25 Joseph believed the promise of God and trusted in His faithfulness. So, Joseph made the sons of Israel swear to bring his bones with them when God brought them out of Egypt to the land He promised to Abraham, Isaac, and Jacob.

Cool Down

Genesis

Major Theological Themes

1. Beginning of Creation (Genesis 1)
2. Beginning of God's People (Genesis 12)
3. Election (Abraham, Isaac, Jacob, Joseph, & Judah)
4. Purpose in Election: God chose them to be a blessing to all nations and all the families of earth
5. Sovereignty
6. Salvation by Grace through Faith (Gospel)
7. Grace and Mercy

Day 5

Read Exodus 1–14

Form Check

Exodus 1:8–22 The situation for the sons of Israel gets a lot more uncomfortable.

Exodus 2 Moses is the author of the Pentateuch and the primary leader until the end of Deuteronomy.

Exodus 2:23–25 Everything is going according to God's plan, for the praise and glory of His name.

Exodus 3 God's declaration of His memorial name will be important to all generations of His people.

Exodus 4:21–23 The sign of the death of the firstborn is declared.

Exodus 4:24–26 Moses is nearly put to death for his failure to keep the covenant. See Genesis 17:10–14.

Exodus 4:31 The people believed and worshipped.

Exodus 5 The people complain against Moses. Moses complains to the Lord.

Exodus 6:1–5 God responds to Moses' complaint. God is revealing Himself to them beyond what He did to their fathers Abraham, Isaac, and Jacob.

Exodus 6:6–7 God declares His plan of deliverance.

Exodus 6:9 The people don't listen to Moses because of their hard circumstances.

Exodus 9:13–16 God's purpose is for the whole earth to know that there is no God like the Lord. His plan is to proclaim His name in all the earth.

Exodus 11:7 God demonstrates the distinction between His people and the rest.

Exodus 12 The Passover is a critically important sign and demonstration. Remember it.

Exodus 12:40–41 The time the sons of Israel lived in Egypt was four hundred thirty years.

Exodus 13:1 Every firstborn belongs to the Lord.

Exodus 13:19 Genesis 50:25 is fulfilled. About four hundred years later.

Exodus 14 God's way was through the sea.

Day 6

Read Exodus 15–27

Form Check

Exodus 15:22–27 Three days after singing of God's deliverance, the people complain of thirst. God miraculously provides water. The people were not far from an oasis. They would have received what they needed in the near future.

Exodus 16:1–3 The people grumble against Moses and Aaron.

Exodus 16:4 God provides manna from heaven and tests the people to see if they will walk in His ways.

Exodus 16:8 Moses explains the grumbling of the people is actually against the Lord.

Exodus 17:3 The people grumble against Moses. Again.

Exodus 19:3–6 God declares His purpose for His people. If they obey Him and keep His covenant, they will be a kingdom of priests and a holy nation.

Exodus 19:10–25 The presence of the Lord is glorious and awesome. It is also dangerous.

Exodus 20 Moses receives the Ten Commandments.

Exodus 23:14–17 God commands the observance of three national feasts. For more on the festivals, read

this article on The Lord's Appointed Times from
fourthyearministries.com.

Exodus 24:12 God promises to give Moses the law
and commandment that God Himself has written for
their instruction.

Exodus 24:13–18 Joshua was with Moses on the
mountain. It is normal for Hebrew narrative to have
people fade into the background. Joshua reemerges
explicitly during Moses's descent (Exodus 32:17).

Exodus 25:9 God commands (and will continue with
every item described) Moses to construct everything
exactly according to the pattern God reveals. Some
readers get bogged down in the details. Don't. God
makes sure that His people are capable of obeying,
even if the particulars are hazy to the modern reader.

Day 7

Read Exodus 28–40

Form Check

Exodus 28:3 God endowed wisdom to perfectly fulfill His command.

Exodus 31:1–11 God gifted individuals with His Spirit to fulfill His instructions.

Exodus 31:18 They were written by God's finger.

Exodus 32:1–6 This incident is important to remember. It is blasphemous idolatry.

Exodus 32:15–16, 19–20 In anger, Moses smashed the tablets that were written upon by God.

Exodus 32:17 Joshua reappears in the narrative. Remember, he's been there all along.

Exodus 32:25–29 The Levites distinguish themselves as being "for the Lord." They become the instrument of God's judgment upon the people.

Exodus 33 Moses understood that God's presence among them was the most important thing.

Exodus 34:27–28 The covenant is renewed. This time, Moses is tasked with writing it down.

Exodus 34:29–35 Moses's nearness to God is emphasized.

Exodus 35:30–35 God enabled them to succeed in the task He gave them.

Exodus 36:6 The people freely and joyously gave. They needed to be restrained from bringing more!

Exodus 39 Note the important repeated phrase "just as the Lord had commanded Moses" (Exodus 39:5, 7, 21, 26, 29, 31–33, 42–43; 40:16, 21).

Exodus 40:33 The work is finished.

Exodus 40:34–38 Everything was leading to this. The glorious presence of God came to dwell in the tabernacle constructed for this very purpose.

Cool Down

Exodus

Major Theological Themes

1. Salvation & Deliverance

2. The Glory of God to the Ends of the Earth

3. The Presence of God Amongst His people

4. Election (Moses; Aaron; Pharaoh; the nation of Israel; Bezalel the son of Uri, the son of Hur; and Oholiab, the son of Ahisamach)

Warm Up

Leviticus

Mind Your Footing

Injuries occur when people don't mind their footing. Tripping during exercise can cause serious injury. Therefore, it is always good to ensure the area is clear of potential stumbling blocks.

Before you get started with Leviticus, we need to remove a few stumbling blocks. Leviticus is easily misunderstood. It is often neglected.

One common stumbling block is the idea that Leviticus is irrelevant for the New Covenant. This is false. However, we don't want to trip over another stumbling block by thinking Christians ought to attempt to practice Levitical law in the modern day. That's a mistake, too.

To properly understand the role and value of Leviticus, we need to ask an important question: Why is this book here?

Exodus ended with the glory of God dwelling among His people. Numbers will pick up the narrative. Yet, Leviticus sits right in the middle. Why?

The answer in one word is: holiness.

God's presence among His people is a dangerous blessing. God is holy. Maintaining the presence of

God is serious business. When taken casually, God's presence broke out in judgment against His people.

As you read Leviticus, pay careful attention to how much blood was shed under the sacrificial system. Notice the importance on maintaining ceremonial cleanness and how easy it was to become ceremonially unclean. Look for the dangers when these things were neglected and/or ignored.

Feel the weight of safely maintaining God's presence amongst His people in the Old Covenant. Then, take some time to rejoice in the glory of what Christ has done. His people enjoy the indwelling presence of the Holy Spirit in the New Covenant. All because of Christ's perfect atoning sacrifice.

If Christians don't read and understand Leviticus, they will misunderstand these important things in the New Testament:

- The holiness of God
- The need for Christ's blood
- The danger and blessing of God's holy presence
- The book of Hebrews

Leviticus is critically important. It's quoted more than most people realize in the New Testament. Read it joyously with this in mind.

Day 8

Read Leviticus 1–14

Form Check

Leviticus 1:3, 10 The sacrifice is to be a male without defect.

Leviticus 2:11 The grain offering shall not contain any leaven.

Leviticus 2:13 Salt must be offered with all of their offerings.

Leviticus 3:1, 6 Male or female without defect.

Leviticus 4—5 Sacrifices for unintentional and/or unknown sins.

Leviticus 9:22–24 God accepts the sacrifice made in accordance with His law.

Leviticus 10 Nadab and Abihu failed to treat God as holy. Judgment was swift and severe.

Day 9

Read Leviticus 15–27

Form Check

Leviticus 16:29–34 The annual atonement is a shadow of the atonement made in and by the promised Christ.

Leviticus 17:14 The blood is identified with its life.

Leviticus 19:2 God commands His people to be holy because He is holy.

Leviticus 19:9–10 God's welfare plan for the poor, needy, and aliens in the nation is declared.

Leviticus 19:18 This is quoted by Jesus. Christ teaches that it is the second greatest commandment.

Leviticus 19:33–34 God commands openness toward strangers and foreigners.

Leviticus 20:26 The people are to be holy because God is holy.

Leviticus 22:17–25 Only flawless animals are acceptable as sacrifices.

Leviticus 23 God commands the observance of His festivals. These are an expansion of the commandments in Exodus 23:14–17. For more, read this article on The Lord's Appointed Times from fourthyearministries.com.

Leviticus 24:17–23 The principle of eye for an eye, tooth for tooth, is explained.

Leviticus 26:1–13 God promises blessing if His people walk in His ways.

Leviticus 26:14–45 Curses and penalties for turning away from the Lord are explained.

For Further Reading You may enjoy reading these related articles from www.theexaltedchrist.com:

- The Holiness Transmitter
- Why Did Jesus Have to Shed His Blood?

Cool Down

Leviticus

Major Theological Themes

1. Worshipping God
2. Bringing in and Maintaining God's Presence
3. The Seriousness of Sin
4. The Price of Redemption (Blood & Sacrifice)
5. God's Appointed Times (Feasts & Festivals)
6. The Levitical Priesthood

Day 10

Read Numbers 1–13

Form Check

Numbers 1:47–54 The importance and danger of bringing the tabernacle with the people.

Numbers 3:25–37 The three divisions of the Levites.

Numbers 3:40–51 The Levites replace the firstborn.

Numbers 4 Remember the duties of the Kohathites. Their duties were intended to prevent death.

Numbers 6:22–27 A famous benediction.

Numbers 7:4–9 Nothing is given to the Kohathites because of the nature of their duty.

Numbers 8:14–22 The Levites belong to God.

Numbers 8:23–26 Retirement plan for the Levites.

Numbers 9:1–14 All are invited to participate.

Numbers 9:12 This ordinance will be fulfilled in the sacrifice of the Lamb of God, Jesus the Christ.

Numbers 9:15–23 They moved with the Lord.

Numbers 12:6–8 God describes how Moses is different than other prophets. Keep this in mind.

Numbers 13 Spying out the Promised Land.

Day 11

Read Numbers 14-26

Form Check

Numbers 14 The people reject God's promise and land. God judges them and promises to raise up a new generation that will take hold of His promise.

Numbers 14:2 The sons of Israel grumble against Moses and Aaron. Again.

Numbers 14:27 God affirms that the grumblings of the people are actually against Him.

Numbers 15:30–31 God deals differently with intentional sin. God calls it blasphemy.

Numbers 15:37–41 Warning against following their own hearts and doing what is right in their own eyes.

Numbers 16:1–40 Korah is cited in the New Testament as an example of what to avoid.

Numbers 16:41 The sons of Israel grumble against Moses and Aaron. Again.

Numbers 18:7 It is dangerous to approach God apart from His defined ways.

Numbers 20:8–13 Moses and Aaron are judged for failing to treat God as holy.

Numbers 21:6–9 Jesus appeals to this event when describing His sacrificial death.

Numbers 22 Balaam's error is warned against in the New Testament.

Numbers 25:10–13 Phinehas's zeal is an important theme to remember.

Day 12

Read Numbers 27–36

Form Check

Numbers 27:15–23 Joshua is commissioned to lead after Moses' death.

Numbers 28:3–8 Offering was made every day in the morning and at twilight. This constantly reminded them, day and night, of the need for blood to be shed to maintain the presence of God in their midst.

Numbers 33:55–56 God warns them in advance of the consequences of disobeying His instructions.

Numbers 34:29 Modern readers think about inheritance differently than it is described in the Old Covenant. The inheritance was the land God gave them, according to the boundaries He established. Even when the inheritance was squandered, there were provisions for the inheritance to be redeemed and/or to be returned during the Jubilee.

Numbers 36:9 No inheritance should be transferred. Each tribe is to hold their own inheritance forever.

Cool Down

Numbers

Major Theological Themes

1. Salvation by Grace (Numbers 21:6–9)
2. God's View of Leadership (Grumbling and Complaining against Moses, Aaron, and the Lord)
3. Consequences of Disobedience
4. God's Faithfulness
5. God's Perfect Vs. Permissive Will (Balaam)
6. Rebellion & Rejection of God's Plan & Inheritance
7. Follow the Lord, Not Your Heart — Do what is right in His sight, not in your own eyes

Day 13

Read Deuteronomy 1–11

Form Check

Deuteronomy 1:26–27 The people were unwilling to receive God's promise.

Deuteronomy 4 Don't add or take away from God's word. Watch yourselves carefully against idolatry.

Deuteronomy 5:6–21 The Ten Commandments.

Deuteronomy 5:33 Walk in the way God has commanded.

Deuteronomy 6:4 The greatest commandment.

Deuteronomy 6:5–25 God's design for households preserving and propagating God's commandments.

Deuteronomy 7:6–11 The reason God loves and chose them.

Deuteronomy 8 Keep the commandments, walk in the ways of God, and fear Him. Don't forget the Lord by not keeping His commandments.

Deuteronomy 10:12 Fear the Lord. Walk in His ways and love Him. Serve the Lord will all your heart and soul.

Deuteronomy 11:22 Walk in all God's ways and hold fast to Him.

Day 14

Read Deuteronomy 12–24

Form Check

Deuteronomy 12:8–9, 28 Be careful to do what is right in the Lord's sight, not your own eyes.

Deuteronomy 13:5 Don't turn from God. The phrase "purge the evil" occurs nine times in today's reading (13:5; 17:7, 12; 19:13, 19; 22:21, 22, 24; and 24:7).

Deuteronomy 16 Remember Exodus 23 and Leviticus 23.

Deuteronomy 17:1 No defects in the sacrifices.

Deuteronomy 18:15–19 God promises a prophet like Moses. Moses was different than other prophets. Review Numbers 12:6–8.

Deuteronomy 19:9 Walk in God's ways. Always.

Deuteronomy 19:14 Don't mess with the inheritance.

Deuteronomy 21:22–23 This law is crucial for understanding why Christ died on the cross.

Deuteronomy 23:3 Remember Genesis 19:36–38.

Deuteronomy 23:14 God walks among His people. Therefore, His people are to be holy.

Day 15

Read Deuteronomy 25–34

Form Check

Deuteronomy 26:16–19 The Lord is God. Walk in His ways.

Deuteronomy 27 The promised curses of God are just as true as the promises of blessing.

Deuteronomy 28 The blessings of obedience and consequences of disobedience to the Old Covenant.

Deuteronomy 28:9 God will establish His people to Himself if they keep His commandments and walk in His ways.

Deuteronomy 29:29 The secret things belong to God. The revealed things belong to His people so that they can observe all His ways.

Deuteronomy 30:15–20 Love God. Walk in His ways. Keep His commandments. Choose life.

Deuteronomy 31:14–22 They will disobey and turn from the Lord despite these stern warnings.

Deuteronomy 32:48–52 The judgment upon Moses is repeated. Remember Numbers 20:8–13.

Deuteronomy 34:5–12 God buried Moses. The Lord knew Moses face to face.

Cool Down

Deuteronomy

Major Theological Themes

1. Renewing the Covenant

2. God's Promises are Multigenerational

3. Blessings of Obedience

4. Curses of Disobedience

5. God Acts for the Glory of His Name — God has done so in the past, God does so in the present, God will do so in the future

Warm Up: The Historical Books

Joshua, Judges, Ruth, Samuel, Kings, Chronicles, Ezra, Nehemiah, & Esther

The historical books cover a period of history spanning approximately 900 years. This lengthy period includes:

- The transition of leadership after Moses to Joshua;
- The time of the Judges;
- The institution of the monarchy;
- The division of the Northern and Southern Kingdoms;
- The eventual fall of both Kingdoms;
- The Babylonian Exile; and
- The return to and rebuilding of Jerusalem.

As you read through these historical books, be aware that Chronicles will cover the same period already covered in Samuel and Kings.

Although the historical period is the same, the Chronicles were written after the return to Jerusalem from the Babylonian Exile. The perspective is very different. This leads to the history being told with different emphases.

Day 16

Read Joshua 1–14

Form Check

Joshua 1:1–9 Leadership has changed. The promise and commands of God are still in effect.

Joshua 2 Rahab, harlot in Jericho, is included in the genealogy of the Christ.

Joshua 5:7 The new generation is circumcised according to the covenant.

Joshua 5:13–15 Joshua asked if the man was for them or for their adversaries. The answer is that he was for the Lord.

Joshua 6 Victory by faith in God's word and ways.

Joshua 6:26 Remember this prophecy.

Joshua 7 Judgment for disobedience to God's word and ways.

Joshua 8:29; 10:26–27 Compare Deuteronomy 21:22–23.

Joshua 8:31–35 Everybody was there. This wouldn't have been a short gathering.

Joshua 10:13 The book of Jashar (alternately, Jasher or Yashar) is a historical book not included in the canon of Scripture.

Day 17

Read Joshua 15—Judges 3

Form Check

Joshua 15:63; 16:10; 17:12–13 Remember Exodus 23:28–33.

Joshua 22:5 Love the Lord. Walk in all His ways. Hold fast to Him with all your heart and soul.

Joshua 23 God's promise is affirmed. God has fulfilled all His promises.

Joshua 24:1–13 History demonstrates God's faithfulness.

Joshua 24:14–28 Serve the Lord. Be faithful. Even if everyone else turns away.

Joshua 24:31 Israel was faithful.

Joshua 24:32 Remember Genesis 50:22–26 and Exodus 13:19.

Judges 2:1–5 Failure to heed the word of the Lord brings consequences.

Judges 2:6–15 A downward spiral.

Judges 2:16–23 A summary of the cycle of apostasy.

Cool Down

Joshua

Major Theological Themes

1. God's Faithfulness

2. God's Holiness

3. Consequences of Disobedience (Personal & National)

4. God's Power to Fulfill His Promises

Day 18

Read Judges 4–16

Form Check

Judges 4:23 God is still working through His people.

Judges 6:13 There are times in history when God's hand is more evident than others.

Judges 7:7 God wanted it to be clear that the victory was from Him.

Judges 8:28–35 God's people must remember to remain faithful and not turn away from the Lord.

Judges 9:23 Look carefully at who sent the evil spirit. God is sovereign and does as He pleases.

Judges 10:6–8 The sons of Israel again turned away from the Lord.

Judges 10:9 The Ammonites originated in Genesis 19:38.

Judges 10:10–16 God's longsuffering and faithful nature are on display.

Judges 13:1 The pattern repeats.

Judges 13:20–23 An appropriate response to being in the presence of the Lord.

Day 19

Read Judges 17—1 Samuel 6

Form Check

Judges 17:6 The reason for the depravity in Israel.

Judges 17:13 Idolatry and adherence are mingled. Micah expects blessing. He should expect judgment.

Judges 19 This depravity is worse than Genesis 19.

Judges 20:16 The amazing accuracy is affirmed with the Hebrew word *chata*. This word is more often translated as sin. Sinning is *missing the mark* that God has declared. Even missing slightly is *sin*.

Judges 21:25 The reason is repeated.

Ruth 1:1 This occurs during the days of the Judges. Boaz was faithful in a time of unfaithfulness.

Ruth 1:4 Ruth is a Moabite. Remember Genesis 19:37 and Deuteronomy 23:3.

Ruth 4:16–22 Ruth, the Moabitess, is part of the lineage of David and the Messiah.

1 Samuel 1:12–16 Things are so poor in Israel that the High Priest can't recognize someone praying.

1 Samuel 2:26 This phrase is very similar to how Jesus is described in Luke 2:52.

1 Samuel 2:22–25 Eli is trying to restore righteousness.

1 Samuel 2:30 God's people are called to walk before Him forever.

1 Samuel 3:19 God is faithful to keep His word.

1 Samuel 4—5 The ark brings judgment instead of blessing.

Cool Down

Judges

Major Theological Themes

1. Apostasy (Turning Away vs. Turning Toward)
2. The Nature and Consequences of Sin and Doing What is Right in our Own Eyes
3. Deliverance
4. Sovereignty of God

Ruth

Major Theological Themes

1. The Kinsmen Redeemer
2. Faithfulness in Unfaithful Times (Remnant)
3. Grafted in to the Covenantal Promise
4. God's Provision
5. The Kingly Lineage of David

Day 20

Read 1 Samuel 7-19

Form Check

1 Samuel 7:15 Samuel was a prophet and a judge.

1 Samuel 8 Israel rejects the Lord and asks for a king. Remember Deuteronomy 17:14–20.

1 Samuel 9:15–17 God selects a Benjamite. Saul's lineage would not reign forever. See Genesis 49:8–10.

1 Samuel 12:12–25 Be diligent to remain faithful.

1 Samuel 12:22 God will not abandon His people on account of His great name.

1 Samuel 12:23 Failure to pray would be sin.

1 Samuel 15:26–28 The kingdom is taken away.

1 Samuel 16:7 God looks to the heart.

1 Samuel 16:14–16, 23 Remember Judges 9:23.

1 Samuel 17:26 David's faith is on display.

1 Samuel 17:41 A crucial detail. Missed by many.

1 Samuel 18:7–8 Praise for David results in Saul's anger burning against David.

1 Samuel 18:10 Remember Judges 9:23 and 1 Samuel 16:14–16.

Day 21

Read 1 Samuel 20—2 Samuel 3

Form Check

1 Samuel 21:1–6 Jesus appeals to this passage in Matthew 12:3–4, Mark 2:25–26, and Luke 6:3–4.

1 Samuel 21:10–15 Praise for David caused this.

1 Samuel 23:2, 4 David inquired of the Lord.

1 Samuel 24 David refuses to act against Saul.

1 Samuel 25:32–39 The Lord acts for David.

1 Samuel 26:23 The Lord will repay.

1 Samuel 28:3–7 Remember Leviticus 19:31; 20:6, 27; and Deuteronomy 18:10–13.

1 Samuel 29 David's reputation causes him trouble.

1 Samuel 30:8 David inquired of the Lord.

1 Samuel 31 The death of Saul and his sons.

2 Samuel 1 David mourns and laments the death of Saul and his house.

2 Samuel 1:18 Remember Joshua 10:13.

2 Samuel 2:1 David inquired of the Lord.

2 Samuel 2:8–11 Saul's son Ish-bosheth is anointed the second king over Israel. Judah followed David.

Day 22

Read 2 Samuel 4-17

Form Check

2 Samuel 4 David mourns Ish-bosheth and puts to death those who killed him.

2 Samuel 5 David is anointed king over all Israel.

2 Samuel 6:3–8 Uh-oh. They failed to remember the important duties from Numbers 4:17–20; 7:6–9. Failure to reverence God and appreciate the danger of His presence led to death.

2 Samuel 7:8–16 God makes a covenantal promise. Terminology of David's descendant being a son of God and God being a father to him is introduced.

2 Samuel 8:13–15 David makes a name for himself and is helped by the Lord.

2 Samuel 11:1 David's sin happens because he is not where he should be. It's the time of year kings go to battle. David sent someone else and stayed home.

2 Samuel 12:24–25 God is a God of redemption.

2 Samuel 15; 16:15–23 Absalom's actions are in fulfillment of God's judgment against David's house in 2 Samuel 12:11.

2 Samuel 17:14 God is sovereignly working through the actions of men.

Day 23

Read 2 Samuel 18—1 Kings 4

Form Check

2 Samuel 18–19 David mourns the death of his treacherous and treasonous son, Absalom.

2 Samuel 21:1 David seeks the presence of the Lord.

2 Samuel 21:18–22 Four sons of the giant are slain. When David fought Goliath (1 Samuel 17) he took five stones, perhaps one for the giant and another for each of his four sons.

2 Samuel 23:1–7 David's last words.

2 Samuel 23:8–39 The mighty men were mighty indeed.

2 Samuel 24:24 David refuses to offer a sacrifice which costs him nothing.

1 Kings 1 Solomon is made king, passing over Adonijah.

1 Kings 2:3 David exhorts Solomon to walk in the ways of the Lord.

1 Kings 3:6–14 Solomon prays for wisdom in leading God's people. God is pleased and calls Solomon to walk and rule in faithfulness before Him.

Cool Down

1 & 2 Samuel

Major Theological Themes

1. The Institution of Israel's Monarchy
2. The Kingly Lineage of David
3. The Son of God & The Davidic Covenant

Day 24

Read 1 Kings 5–15

Form Check

1 Kings 5:2–6 Solomon seeks to build the temple after his father, David, was not allowed to.

1 Kings 6:11–13 God promises to keep His word if Solomon will walk in the ways of the Lord.

1 Kings 7 Solomon's palace is significantly larger than the temple described in 1 Kings 6.

1 Kings 8:23–25 God is faithful to His servants who walk before Him.

1 Kings 8:41–43 Solomon prays that God's name will be glorified to the ends of the earth.

1 Kings 8:61 Be wholly devoted to the Lord. Walk in all His ways.

1 Kings 9:3–9 God warns against apostasy.

1 Kings 11:1–13 Solomon turns away from God.

1 Kings 11:33 Judgment declared upon those who have forsaken Him and have not walked in His ways.

1 Kings 12 The kingdom is divided.

1 Kings 12:25–33 This sinful act will influence the northern kingdom of Israel for its entire existence. Remember the sin and idolatry of Jeroboam.

1 Kings 13:33–34 Jeroboam does not heed the call to repentance.

1 Kings 14:7–16 Consequences of Jeroboam's sin declared.

1 Kings 14:19 This phrase "the Book of the Chronicles" is not referring to the books 1 & 2 Chronicles in Scripture. This phrase occurs 36 times in the NASB. There were additional, non-scriptural, records kept for kings of Israel, Judah, and other nations that are not included in your Bible. These are what are being referenced.

1 Kings 14:21–24 Rehoboam leads Judah astray.

1 Kings 15:1–5 Contrast is made between walking in sin and walking in devotion to the Lord. God intercedes because of His promise to David.

1 Kings 15:8–14 A good king in Judah with a heart wholly devoted to the Lord.

1 Kings 15:29–34 Jeroboam's sin continues to have consequences.

Day 25

Read 1 Kings 16—2 Kings 5

Form Check

1 Kings 16:1–3 Walking in the sin of Jeroboam continues to wreak havoc.

1 Kings 16:18–19 Consequences of walking in the way of Jeroboam.

1 Kings 16:21 Two kings in Israel.

1 Kings 16:26 Omri did not walk with the Lord but in the way of Jeroboam.

1 Kings 16:31 It is not trivial to walk in the sins of Jeroboam.

1 Kings 16:34 Fulfillment of Joshua 6:26.

1 Kings 18:1, 36–46 Elijah's prayer is used as a model in the New Testament (James 5:17–18).

1 Kings 20:11 This is sound advice.

1 Kings 21:21–22 Idolatry provokes God to anger.

1 Kings 21:25–26 Ahab sold himself to do evil.

1 Kings 22:20–23 Remember Judges 9:23 and 1 Samuel 16:14–16.

1 Kings 22:37–38 Elijah's prophecy from 1 Kings 21:19 is fulfilled.

1 Kings 22:41–46 Another good king in Judah.

1 Kings 22:51–53 God again provoked by wicked leaders walking in the way of Jeroboam.

2 Kings 2:11–12 Elijah was taken to heaven alive. Remember Genesis 5:24.

2 Kings 3:1–3 More consequences for those who cling to idolatry and the sin of Jeroboam.

Day 26

Read 2 Kings 6-20

Form Check

2 Kings 7:16–20 Elisha's prophecy was fulfilled exactly.

2 Kings 8:19 God is faithful to His promise.

2 Kings 9:33–37 Elijah's prophecy from 1 Kings 21:23 is fulfilled.

2 Kings 10:29–31 Jehu was not careful to walk with the Lord. He walked in the sin of Jeroboam.

2 Kings 11 Athaliah, Queen of Judah.

2 Kings 12:1–3 Another good king in Judah.

2 Kings 13:1–13 Two more kings walk in the sin of Jeroboam.

2 Kings 14:23–29 Another Jeroboam reigns. Despite the victories he achieved, he did evil by failing to depart from the sin of Jeroboam like the rest.

2 Kings 15 Four more kings do evil by walking in the sin of Jeroboam in Israel. Two more kings do right in the Lord's sight in Judah.

2 Kings 16:1–4 Ahaz, king of Judah, walks in the ways of the kings of Israel.

2 Kings 17:7–23 God judged the kingdom of Israel because they did not depart from the sin of Jeroboam until the Lord removed them from His sight.

2 Kings 17:19 Judah did not walk with the Lord, but turned away from Him and walked in the customs introduced to them by Israel.

2 Kings 18:4 Remember Numbers 21:6–9. Hezekiah ended idolatry that had endured for centuries.

2 Kings 18:5–7 Hezekiah trusted and clung to the Lord. The Lord was with him.

2 Kings 19:1–2 Hezekiah, Eliakim, and Isaiah. You'll read about all of these men again in Isaiah.

2 Kings 20:16–19 The word of the Lord will be fulfilled.

Day 27

Read 2 Kings 21—1 Chronicles 8

Form Check

2 Kings 21:1–18 Manasseh was a wicked king in Judah. To say the least.

2 Kings 21:19–22 Amon walked in the ways of his fathers, not in the ways of the Lord. By doing so, Amon forsook the Lord.

2 Kings 22:1–13 Because of Josiah's reforms, the book of the law was found. Even more importantly, it was read and obeyed.

2 Kings 23:1–3 The people covenant with Josiah to walk with the Lord.

2 Kings 23:15 King Josiah finally tore down the altar at Bethel which Jeroboam had erected. This altar had caused sin from beginning to end of the kingdom of Israel.

2 Kings 23:21–27 Passover celebrated again. Josiah turned to the Lord with all his heart, soul, and mind. Still, God's wrath burned against Judah because of Manasseh. Josiah is Judah's last good king before judgment comes from Babylon.

2 Kings 24:17–18 The king of Babylon appoints the king in Jerusalem. This was Jehoiachin's uncle, not the uncle of the king of Babylon.

2 Kings 25 Judgment from God at the hands of the Babylonians.

1 Chronicles 1—8 Remember: Chronicles was written after the people returned to their land at the end of the Babylonian exile. Although the temple and city had been destroyed, God's promises were still in effect. These promises depended on the lineages that God had chosen. If you're excited about salvation by the grace of God through faith in the Messiah, then you should be excited to see God faithfully preserved these lines according to His promise.

Cool Down

1 & 2 Kings

Major Theological Themes

1. Blessing for Obedience
2. Curses for Disobedience
3. The Dangers of Idolatry
4. God's Loving Call to Repentance
5. God's Patience

Day 28

Read 1 Chronicles 9–25

Form Check

1 Chronicles 9:1 After God's faithfulness in preserving a remnant is told through the genealogies, the people are reminded that their judgment came because of their unfaithfulness.

1 Chronicles 10:13–14 Saul was judged for failing to keep the word of the Lord.

1 Chronicles 11:1–3 David is anointed according to the word of the Lord through Samuel.

1 Chronicles 14:3–4 David's great sin with Bathsheba is not mentioned.

1 Chronicles 15:2, 13 David learned from the death of Uzza (2 Chronicles 13:7–14). Compare 2 Samuel 6.

1 Chronicles 16:7 Asaph is assigned to give thanks to the Lord. There are twelve psalms attributed to Asaph: Psalm 50, and Psalms 73—83.

1 Chronicles 17:7–15 The Davidic covenant.

1 Chronicles 17:19–22 God made a people for Himself and for the sake of His great name.

1 Chronicles 22:8–10 David is not allowed to build the temple because he is a man of war.

Day 29

Read 1 Chronicles 26—2 Chronicles 10

Form Check

1 Chronicles 28:2–3 David was not allowed to build the temple because he shed so much blood.

1 Chronicles 28:9–10 God searches all hearts and understands every intent. Don't forsake Him.

1 Chronicles 29:10–20 Lord, glorify Your name. Direct the hearts of Your people to You.

2 Chronicles 5:13–14 The glory of the Lord fills the temple.

2 Chronicles 6:14–16 Solomon affirms God's covenant faithfulness toward those who walk with Him.

2 Chronicles 6:32–33 May all the peoples of earth know the Lord and fear Him.

2 Chronicles 7:1–3 Truly He is good. Truly His lovingkindness lasts forever.

2 Chronicles 7:17–22 Walk before the Lord. Don't forsake Him.

2 Chronicles 9:13–30 Solomon's wealth is hard to imagine. Silver wasn't even considered valuable during his reign. Even billionaires today would consider silver as having some value.

Day 30

Read 2 Chronicles 11–23

Form Check

2 Chronicles 11:14–17 The sin of Jeroboam is briefly mentioned. Chronicles prioritizes the southern kingdom of Judah. The northern kingdom of Israel is pushed to the background.

2 Chronicles 13 War between Israel and Judah.

2 Chronicles 14—16 Three chapters on King Asa. Only seventeen verses about Asa in 1 Kings 15:8–24.

2 Chronicles 18:1 A good king in Judah allied himself by marriage to a wicked king in Israel.

2 Chronicles 18:20–23 Remember Judges 9:23, 1 Samuel 16:14–16, and 1 Kings 22:20–23.

2 Chronicles 19:1–4 Jehoshaphat rebuked for his alliance with the wicked king of Israel. Reforms follow.

2 Chronicles 20:5–12 Jehoshaphat leads the whole nation in prayer before the Lord. Everyone was there with their wives, infants, and children.

2 Chronicles 21:4–20 Jehoram did not walk with the Lord but in the ways of wickedness. This turning away from the Lord was rebuked and resulted in painful judgment.

Be Encouraged

Great job so far! You are a third of the way done.
Keep it up. Don't slow down. Be strong and
courageous.

9 Sing to Him, sing praises to Him;
Speak of all His wonders.
10 Glory in His holy name;
Let the heart of those who seek the LORD be glad.
11 Seek the LORD and His strength;
Seek His face continually.
12 Remember His wonderful deeds which
He has done,
His marvels and the judgments from His mouth.

−1 Chronicles 16:9–12

Day 31

Read 2 Chronicles 24-36

Form Check

2 Chronicles 24:20-22 Jesus speaks of this while rebuking the Pharisees (Matthew 23:35; Luke 11:51).

2 Chronicles 25:2 God looks to the heart.

2 Chronicles 25:15, 20, 27 God sovereignly works through the actions of men.

2 Chronicles 26:16 Be careful of pride. It can cause people to act corruptly.

2 Chronicles 28:1-5 God handed His people over to judgment when they turned away from Him.

2 Chronicles 28:22 King Ahaz became more unfaithful in his time of distress.

2 Chronicles 30:7-9 Do not be like those who stiffened their necks and hardened their hearts. Return to the Lord so that He may be gracious and compassionate.

2 Chronicles 31:20-21 Hezekiah sought the Lord in every work with all his heart.

2 Chronicles 33:12-13 In his distress, Manasseh humbled himself and turned to the Lord.

2 Chronicles 36:20-23 The Lord kept His word.

Cool Down

1 & 2 Chronicles

Major Theological Themes

1. God's Faithfulness to Keep His Promises

2. Exile & Restoration

3. Davidic Line and Promises Remain

4. Temple Worship

5. God's Name being made Holy among the Nations

Day 32

Read Ezra 1–10

Form Check

Ezra 1:1–2 God is sovereign over all nations.

Ezra 2:2 The return was led by Zerubbabel.

Ezra 3:8 The temple restoration begins.

Ezra 3:10–13 Mixed emotions and responses at the laying of the foundation for the second temple.

Ezra 6:14–15 The temple is successfully completed thanks to the prophesying of Haggai and Zechariah.

Ezra 6:19 The Passover is observed.

Ezra 7:1 Ezra comes up to Jerusalem.

Ezra 7:10 Ezra set his heart to study the law. To practice it himself. And to teach it to others.

Ezra 8:22–23 God's favor is toward earnest seekers; His power and anger against all who forsake Him.

Ezra 9:3 Ezra pulls out his own hair in his distress.

Ezra 9:5–15 Corporate confession of sin and guilt.

Ezra 10:1 Men, women and children gathered together.

Day 33

Read Nehemiah 1–13

Form Check

Nehemiah 1 Nehemiah is moved. He prays according to God's revealed will and ways.

Nehemiah 2:4 Nehemiah prays quickly while speaking to King Artaxerxes.

Nehemiah 3 Everyone was involved in the project. Many of the repairs are made in close proximity to the house of the worker. They were personally invested in the success of the project.

Nehemiah 5:9 Nehemiah rebukes and encourages the people to walk in the fear of their God.

Nehemiah 6:16 It was clear to all that God was involved.

Nehemiah 8:1–8 A model of expository preaching. All were present.

Nehemiah 9 History is reviewed to see God's faithfulness throughout His dealings with His people.

Nehemiah 10:28–31 The people take upon themselves both a curse and an oath to walk in God's ways and according to His commandments.

Nehemiah 13:25 Nehemiah pulls out the hair of others in his distress.

Cool Down

Ezra & Nehemiah

Major Theological Themes

1. God's Sovereignty
2. God's Mercy
3. Repentance
4. God Answers Prayer
5. Godly Leadership

Day 34

Read Esther 1–10

Form Check

Esther 1:1–4 This is taking place in Susa, the capitol city of the Media-Persian empire. King Ahasuerus is also mentioned in Ezra 4:6. Some had returned to Jerusalem. Esther is about faithful Jews who were still scattered among the nations.

Esther 2:5–7 Mordecai was taken into exile with Jeconiah. He was now raising Hadassah (Esther) in Susa as his adopted daughter.

Esther 2:21–23 The significance of this event will be revealed later.

Esther 4:14 Mordecai affirms that deliverance will come from somewhere. He also affirms the importance and consequences of Esther's actions and potential inactions.

Esther 7:9–10 Compare Psalm 7:15–16.

Esther 9:20–22 A new holiday is declared and celebrated to commemorate their deliverance.

Did you notice? God was never explicitly mentioned in the entire book of Esther. However, it is clear that God is sovereignly working in the details to arrange for the deliverance of His people from the schemes of their enemies.

Cool Down

Esther

Major Theological Themes

1. God's Providence and Sovereignty
2. God Opposes the Proud
3. Fear God, Not Man

Warm Up: The Poetic Books

Job, Psalms, Proverbs, Ecclesiastes, & Song of Solomon

Wisdom is associated both with old age and intellect today. That is not the case with these poetic books in Scripture. A better way to understand scriptural wisdom is: skillful living. It is the proper application of God's revealed principles in your daily life.

Hebrew wisdom is realistic, not idealistic. Wise living doesn't guarantee favorable circumstances. The encouragement is to live wisely anyway.

To understand the truth that is being communicated we need to understand the style of communication. The style is drastically different than the historical narrative sections you just finished.

These books are filled with parallelism, hyperbole, emotion, metaphor, and are often written in a way that is intended to be memorable.

As we follow the canonical order it is important to understand that these poetic books do not follow chronologically after the historical books. They need to be overlaid and filtered into the history we've already read in the Old Testament.

Day 35

Read Job 1–14

Form Check

Job 1—2 This opening narrative sets important context necessary to understand what follows.

Job 1:1 The events recorded about Job are very early historically. They are likely occurring before Abraham was called by God in Genesis 12.

Job 1:8; 2:3 God affirms Job is a righteous man. Job's righteousness is called into question by others in the book. This opening section tells us the truth.

Job 1:9–11; 2:5 Satan incorrectly asserts that Job worships God only because he is blessed by God. God asserts that Satan is wrong, knowing Job worships Him because He is worthy.

Job 1:13–19 Satan shows no mercy. He is able to work through humans, natural, and even supernatural means.

Job 1:20 Job responds by worshipping the Lord.

Job 2:11–13 Job's friends show compassion and sit with him for a week before speaking.

Job 3 The cycle of speeches begins.

Day 36

Read Job 15–28

Form Check

Job 16:1–5 Job tells his friends they are lousy comforters. It is easy to criticize someone in his situation. They are wrongly asserting that God is punishing Job for doing something wrong.

Job 16:21 Job wants to make his case to God. He will rethink this position later on.

Job 19:7–20 Job describes his sorry situation in vivid terms.

Job 19:25–27 Job asserts his hope in God.

Job 23:11–12 Could you describe your own walk with God in this way?

Job 23:13–14 God is sovereign. He does as He pleases.

Job 28:12–28 True wisdom is incredibly valuable. It is to fear the Lord and to depart from evil.

Day 37
Read Job 29-42

Form Check

Job 31:1 A wise covenant to make.

Job 32 A new figure emerges: Elihu.

Job 38 God enters into the conversation in a whirlwind. For the next four chapters God describes His power, knowledge, and glory.

Job 42:2 God can do all things. No plan of His can be thwarted.

Job 42:5–6 Hearing about the Lord and beholding Him are not the same things.

Job 42:7 God addresses Eliphaz the Temanite and his two friends (Bildad the Shuhite and Zophar the Naamathite). Interestingly, God is silent about what Elihu had to say.

Job 42:10–17 Some think the point of this book is that God will bring about double blessing after trial. However, this is a grave misunderstanding. Job worshipped God because God is worthy. No matter what. Even after this severe trial, Job would have mourned the loss of his first ten children. What Job lost was real. Irreplaceable. What Job always had (and never lost) was an understanding the God is God. We, too, should worship God because of who He is, not because of what we want Him to give us.

Cool Down

Job

Major Theological Themes

1. God's Glory and Worthiness to be Worshipped
2. Theodicy (that is, an explanation of why evil and suffering exist in the world)
3. The Reality of Evil and Satan
4. The Sovereignty of God

Day 38

Read Psalm 1–18

Form Check

Psalm 1 The righteous person is like a tree that brings forth fruit in its season. The Lord knows the way of the righteous. The way of the wicked is death.

Psalm 2 A psalm about the Messiah in His current exalted position. Psalm 2:10–12 is worth memorizing. Don't perish under the wrath of the Son. Take refuge in Him instead.

Psalm 4:2–5 Tremble. Do not sin. Trust in the Lord.

Psalm 5:4–6 Many don't believe this is true about God. But here it is, in God's word. Why do you think Psalm 5:5 isn't seen on bumper stickers or refrigerator magnets?

Psalm 7:11–12 This imagery is about God being ready to destroy the unrepentant. A God who is angry about sin every day.

Psalm 8 God's majesty and greatness are declared.

Psalm 11:7 The Lord is righteous. God loves righteousness. The upright will behold His face.

Psalm 16:10 A messianic prophecy declaring the resurrection of the Christ.

Day 39

Read Psalm 19-33

Form Check

Psalm 19 God's creation declares His glory. God's word is more valuable than gold and sweeter than honey. Verse 14 is worth praying every day.

Psalm 22 Jesus quoted this psalm from the cross. It explains why the Son was forsaken by the Father on the cross. It wasn't for the reasons the Pharisees wanted Him executed. It was for the glory of God.

Psalm 23 Perhaps the most famous Psalm.

Psalm 24 Who is this King of glory? The Lord strong and mighty. He is the King of glory.

Psalm 29 Ascribe to the Lord the glory due His name. He is King forever.

Psalm 32:1–2 This psalm is quoted in the New Testament regarding the blessing of salvation. Salvation is about the forgiveness of our sins.

Psalm 33:18–22 The eye of the Lord is on people who fear Him. Rejoice in Him. Trust in His holy name.

Day 40

Read Psalm 34-47

Form Check

Psalm 40:6–8 Quoted in the New Testament of the Messiah (Hebrews 10:5–10).

Psalm 40:9–10 Proclaim the glad tidings of salvation. Don't restrain your lips. Don't hide God's righteousness in your heart. Speak openly of God's faithfulness and His salvation.

Psalm 41:9 A messianic prophecy. Fulfilled in the betrayal of Christ by Judas.

End of Book 1 The collection of psalms in the Scripture is divided into five books. The first book is Psalm 1—41. Book 2 is Psalm 42—72. Speculative reasons have been given for this arrangement. It is good to be aware, but it is unwise to be dogmatic about the reasons for the divisions into these groups.

Psalm 42 Of the sons of Korah. Some people think every psalm was written by David. They weren't.

Psalm 44 Another psalm by the sons of Korah. Verse 22 is quoted by Paul in Romans 8:36.

Psalm 45:6–7 A messianic psalm. Quoted in Hebrews 1:8–9.

Psalm 47 God is the King of all the earth.

Day 41

Read Psalm 48–62

Form Check

Psalm 50 A psalm of Asaph. God tells the wicked (50:16–21) they have no right to take His name or covenant on their lips. Their mistake was that they thought God was like them. He isn't.

Psalm 51 David's psalm of repentance after his sin with Bathsheba. David wants to be right with God so he can lead others to be right with God.

Psalm 52:6–7 In the end, it is laughable to live a life trusting in riches and pursuing evil desires. Yet, many foolishly do it anyway.

Psalm 53:1–3 This psalm is quoted in Romans 3.

Psalm 55:16–23 Cast your burden upon the Lord. God will not allow the righteous to be shaken.

Psalm 56:13 Deliverance was given so that David could walk with his God.

Psalm 57 Be exalted, O God, above the heavens. May Your glory be known in all the earth!

Psalm 62 Salvation is from the Lord. Trust in Him at all times.

Day 42

Read Psalm 63-75

Form Check

Psalm 64:9–10 All people will fear the Lord, declare His work, and contemplate His glorious deeds.

Psalm 65:4 How blessed is the one that God chooses to bring near to Himself and to dwell in His presence!

Psalm 66 Shout joyfully and bless the Lord for all His goodness and faithfulness.

Psalm 67 God bless us, so that all the people of the earth will know You and Your ways and will fear Your holy name.

Psalm 68:18 The Lord is worthy to receive gifts from men. The Apostle Paul makes the astonishing claim that, although Christ is worthy to receive gifts, He actually *gave* gifts to His church when He ascended (Ephesians 4:11–16).

Psalm 69 Entrust yourself to the Lord.

Psalm 72 A Psalm of Solomon.

End of Book 2 Book 3 is comprised of Psalm 73—89. Psalm 73—83 are attributed to Asaph.

Psalm 73 Many can relate to Asaph's potential stumbling block over the prosperity of the wicked. The turning point begins in verse 17.

Day 43

Read Psalm 76-88

Form Check

Psalm 77:19 God's ways are not our ways. His way was in the sea. Remember Exodus 14:13–31.

Psalm 78 God's faithfulness over history is declared.

Psalm 78:5–17 Asaph speaks of the importance of faithfulness in the family. God commands His people to instruct their children to walk with God and to remember Him in all their ways. When the people are unfaithful, they forget and turn away from Him.

Psalm 79:9 Asaph prays for God to act for the glory and sake of God's great name.

Psalm 81:11–13 God gave His people over *after* they refused to obey Him. God affirms His desire that His people would walk with Him.

Psalm 82:6 Jesus quotes this verse in John 10:34.

Psalm 83:13–18 Act, Lord, that they may seek You.

Psalm 84:10–12 The sons of Korah declare God's goodness to those who walk uprightly before Him.

Psalm 86 All nations will worship the Lord and glorify His name. He alone is God.

Psalm 88 The saddest psalm. It never turns positive.

Day 44

Read Psalm 89–102

Form Check

Psalm 89 Attributed to Ethan the Ezrahite.

End of Book 3 Book 4 is Psalm 90—106.

Psalm 90 A Prayer of Moses. Teach us to number our days and live each day for Your eternal glory.

Psalm 91 This messianic psalm is used by Satan in the wilderness. Satan tries to tempt Christ to test the Lord instead of trusting in Him.

Psalm 92 A song for the Sabbath.

Psalm 94 The Lord is a God of vengeance and the Judge of the earth.

Psalm 95 The Lord is a great God and King above all gods. Verse 11 is cited in Hebrews 4. Don't harden your heart. Don't turn away from the Lord.

Psalm 96 Proclaim salvation and the deeds of the Lord each day. Tell the nations that the Lord reigns. Declare that the Lord is coming to judge the earth.

Psalm 100 A Psalm for thanksgiving. Not for the North American holiday, but for giving thanks any time.

Day 45

Read Psalm 103–117

Form Check

Psalm 103:6–14 Thank the Lord for His grace and compassion toward us!

Psalm 103:19 God's sovereignty and kingdom rules over all.

Psalm 104:9 God established the boundaries of the seas.

Psalm 105:1–7 Make the deeds of the Lord known. Seek His face continually.

Psalm 106:19–21 This is very similar to how Paul defines sin in Romans 1:22–23. Don't exchange the glory of God for a lie. Don't forget God your Savior.

Psalm 106:30–31 Remember Numbers 25:10–13.

End of Book 4 Book 5 is Psalm 107—150.

Psalm 109:8 This verse is quoted in Acts 1:20 about filling Judas' vacant apostolic office.

Psalm 110 Remember Genesis 14:17–24. Verses 5–7 describe Christ's second coming in wrath to destroy His enemies before ushering in His kingdom of peace. This imagery will be seen again in Revelation.

Day 46

Read Psalm 118–130

Form Check

Psalm 118 A messianic psalm. Christ is the stone the builders rejected. Let us rejoice and be glad.

Psalm 119 The longest psalm and longest chapter in Scripture. It is an acrostic psalm. Each line of every stanza begins with the next letter of the Hebrew alphabet. This is lost in translation but explains why each section is headed with a different Hebrew letter in our English translations. It is a celebration of God's word, law, testimonies, and commandments.

Psalms 120—134 Songs of Ascents. These were intended to be sung on the way to gather to worship the Lord.

Psalm 121 Look to the Lord. He is our keeper.

Psalm 123 Look to the Lord, until He is gracious to you.

Psalm 125 Those who trust in the Lord cannot be moved.

Psalm 126 The Lord has done great things for us.

Psalm 128 How blessed is everyone who fears the Lord and who walks in His ways.

Day 47

Read Psalm 131-145

Form Check

Psalm 132:11–12 The Lord has sworn, He will not turn back.

Psalm 133:1 How good and pleasant it is to dwell together in unity with other believers!

Psalm 135:6 The Lord is sovereign in all the earth. He does as He pleases.

Psalm 137 Looking back upon the judgment brought upon God's people during Babylonian captivity.

Psalm 138 The Lord is exalted. All the kings of the earth will give thanks and sing of His ways.

Psalm 139 The Lord is all-knowing. Lead us in the everlasting way, oh Lord.

Psalm 141 Look to the Lord. Take refuge in Him.

Psalm 143:2 No one is righteous according to God's perfect standard. This explains our need for a perfect Savior.

Psalm 143:8–12 Teach me the way I should walk. Teach me to do Your will. You are my God. I am Your servant.

Psalm 145:17–21 Call upon the Lord in truth.

Day 48

Read Psalm 146—Proverbs 9

Form Check

Psalm 146:8 The Lord loves the righteous.

Psalm 147:11 The Lord favors those who fear Him and who wait for His lovingkindness.

Psalm 148 The Lord alone is exalted. His glory is above earth and heaven. Praise Him!

What are proverbs? The power of a proverb is found in the concise, memorable formulation. They express generalized truth. Proverbs must be interpreted as proverbial and poetic statements. Sometimes these generalized truths are told from opposite perspectives. This may seem, initially, contradictory. Upon reflection, the wisdom each proverb imparts becomes clearer.

Proverbs 1:1–7 The purpose of the collection of Proverbs is explained in these opening verses. It begins with the fear of the Lord. Receive these sayings, don't despise them.

Proverbs 1—9 The first nine chapters of Proverbs form a major unit. The pursuit of wisdom is encouraged. The danger of folly is exposed.

Cool Down

Psalms

Major Theological Themes
1. Worship of God
2. Praise God — Israel and the Nations
3. God's Attributes, Character, and Worthiness
4. A Theology of Song

The Power of Song

Songs are easy to remember and difficult to forget. Songs can be influential and powerful, both for good and ill. God's people often forget Him and His commands. Song offers a helpful solution to this ongoing problem. Scriptural examples include:

- Exodus 15:1–21
- Deuteronomy 31:14—32:43
- Ephesians 5:19
- Colossians 3:16
- Acts 16:24–26
- Matthew 26:30
- Mark 14:26

It is likely not coincidence that the longest book is Psalms (150 chapters) and the longest chapter is also a psalm (Psalm 119).

With this in mind, it is wise to consider what songs we choose to fill our hearts and minds with.

Day 49

Read Proverbs 10–21

Form Check

Proverbs 10—24 These chapters are a collection of the proverbs of Solomon.

Proverbs 10:2 Righteousness delivers from death.

Proverbs 10:27 The fear of the Lord extends life.

Proverbs 11:1 Dishonesty in business is an abomination to God.

Proverbs 11:4 Riches are worthless on Judgment Day.

Proverbs 12:10 A righteous person will express compassion towards all of creation.

Proverbs 12:22 Lying is an abomination to God.

Proverbs 14:4 The easy way is often not the best way.

Proverbs 14:31 Honor the Lord by being generous.

Proverbs 15:3 The Lord sees everything.

Proverbs 16:2 Only the Lord's assessment matters.

Proverbs 16:20 Pay attention. It's worth it!

Proverbs 20:2 Provoking a king is a bad idea.

Day 50

Read Proverbs 22–31

Form Check

Proverbs 22:6 Many have heard this promise. It is also a warning.

Proverbs 23:4–5 It is foolish to weary yourself to gain wealth. There are more worthwhile pursuits.

Proverbs 23:17 Don't envy sinners.

Proverbs 25—29 Another collection of Solomon's proverbs.

Proverbs 25:7 Jesus teaches a similar parable to this in Luke 14:7–11.

Proverbs 26:4–5 These two thoughts are complementary, not contradictory. They teach truth from different perspectives.

Proverbs 26:18–19 Don't be a like a madman throwing firebrands, arrows and death.

Proverbs 28:1 The righteous are as bold as a lion.

Proverbs 30:1 The words of Agur.

Proverbs 31:1 The words of Lemuel.

Cool Down

Proverbs

Major Theological Themes

1. Wisdom Vs. Folly
2. Character Formation

Day 51

Read Ecclesiastes 1–12

Form Check

A Controversial Book Ecclesiastes is easy to misunderstand. Especially if you don't read it all in one sitting. Similar to some of the comments of Job's friends, there are statements in this book that are not meant to be taken as truth. The context helps us to interpret what is wisdom and what is folly.

Ecclesiastes 1:1–2 The book begins by speaking of the Preacher in third person and with the famous catchphrase. This serves as an opening bookend.

Ecclesiastes 3:11—6:12 This central unit would have stood out to the original hearers.

Ecclesiastes 10:19 This idea, for example, is intended to be understood as foolishness. Compare to Ecclesiastes 5:10 in the main central unit.

Ecclesiastes 12:8 The closing bookend. Notice that the Preacher is again referred to in third person with the famous catchphrase.

Ecclesiastes 12:9–14 The conclusion. This explains the intent of this book. Everything should be interpreted in light of this conclusion.

Cool Down

Ecclesiastes

Major Theological Themes

1. The Fear of the Lord
2. Wisdom Vs. Folly
3. Life is Good

Day 52

Read Song of Solomon 1-8

Form Check

Another Controversial Book Many have twisted this important book. They've made it something it was never intended to be. As you read this book, from beginning to end, it should be clear what it is about.

Talking about sex in the church makes some people uncomfortable. It is my opinion that this discomfort has caused some to attempt to make Song of Solomon more "appropriate." So, they spiritualize it. They make it about something other than sexual intimacy between a husband and wife.

Twisting and obscuring the intended message doesn't purify it. Ironically, it corrupts the book.

If the church pushes sexual morality into darkness, or ignores it, we shouldn't be surprised when people plunge headlong into sexual immorality in the world.

Human sexuality is the most powerful creative force on earth. It is the process by which new human beings are created. Accordingly, it can be one of the most destructive forces when it is abused.

God, in His goodness, has included a book about sexual morality in the Bible. Song of Solomon is it.

Cool Down

Song of Solomon

Major Theological Theme

1. Sexual Morality

Warm Up: The Major Prophetic Books

Isaiah, Jeremiah, Lamentations, Ezekiel, & Daniel

The remainder of the Old Testament is the prophetic books. These are sometimes called the "writing prophets." All of them were written between 900—400 BC.

These books are not arranged chronologically. They are lumped into two broad groups:

- The Major Prophets
- The Minor Prophets

These terms do not reflect importance. It is from the Latin *majoris* and *minoris*, referring to their length.

The Major Prophets will cover the time span from King Uzziah's reign through the Babylonian Exile.

Prophetic ministry, whether Major or Minor, writing or non-writing, may be summarized as reminding and enforcing the covenant.

Prophetic utterance is built off of the foundation of God's promises made to the fathers. The prophets are not primarily declaring new information. They are repeating what has already been declared. They are calling people to repentance and faithfulness.

Day 53

Read Isaiah 1–15

Form Check

Isaiah 1:1 Isaiah's ministry was during the reigns of Uzziah, Jotham, Ahaz, and Hezekiah, kings of Judah. It may be helpful to review 2 Kings 15—20 and 2 Chronicles 26—32 to remember this period.

Isaiah 2:2–4 The nations will come to the Lord in the future. They will desire to walk in His ways.

Isaiah 6 A glorious vision accompanies Isaiah's call. His ministry is explained. It is not going to be easy.

Isaiah 7—8 A well-known prophecy about the virgin who will be with child. This prophecy was fulfilled within the immediate context (8:3) as a sign for that generation. It also looks forward to the birth of Christ, for which it is better known.

Isaiah 9:1—7 A prophecy concerning the coming Prince of Peace. This is built on the promise made to David, is fulfilled in Jesus of Nazareth, and is accomplished by the zeal of the Lord.

Isaiah 10 God is sovereign over Assyria. This is the nation God used to discipline Israel and which God delivered Judah and King Hezekiah from.

Isaiah 11:1–5 The character of the Messiah is described.

Isaiah 11:6—12:6 The coming kingdom of the Messiah is described in beautiful detail.

Isaiah 13—23 This section is sometimes referred to as the book of the nations. God is sovereign over all the nations of earth.

Isaiah 14:3–21 This passage is explicitly about the king of Babylon. However, many theologians use this passage to go beyond the human ruler to also be a description of the characteristics of Satan.

Day 54

Read Isaiah 16–31

Form Check

Isaiah 19:19–25 The reach of salvation will include even the most vicious enemies of Israel: Egypt and Assyria.

Isaiah 22:20–25 The key of David. Remember Eliakim from Hezekiah's reign. Compare Revelation 3:7. For more on this important passage, listen to this sermon preached at Howell Bible Church (www.howellbible.org/sermons) on May 27, 2018, entitled: The Key of David.

Isaiah 25 A song of praise because of God's faithfulness. Let us rejoice and be glad in His salvation.

Isaiah 28 God declares that He is laying in Zion a tested and costly foundation. This is fulfilled in the Messiah, Jesus. God promises that the one who believes will not be disturbed.

Isaiah 30:18 God longs to be gracious. Turn to Him in humble faith.

Isaiah 31:6–7 Those who have turned away from God are called to repent and return to Him.

Isaiah 31:8–9 Fulfilled in Isaiah 37:36–38.

Day 55

Read Isaiah 32-43

Form Check

Isaiah 33:5-6 The Lord is exalted. The fear of the Lord is a treasure.

Isaiah 33:22 The Lord is judge, lawgiver, and king. He alone is able to save us.

Isaiah 35 The coming kingdom is declared.

Isaiah 37 Remember Isaiah 31:8-9.

Isaiah 40 The tone of Isaiah radically changes in this chapter. Some assert that the material that follows is the work of another author. This is unnecessary. The simplest explanation is that the focus has changed, which results in a change of tone.

Isaiah 40:3 A prophecy fulfilled by John the Baptist.

Isaiah 40:8 The word of God stands forever.

Isaiah 40:9-10 Here is your God. Awesome in power. Tender in His care for His flock.

Isaiah 41 God is the first and the last. He is the Redeemer.

Isaiah 42 God promises justice to the nations. This will be fulfilled in the righteous reign of the Messiah.

Day 56

Read Isaiah 44-57

Form Check

Isaiah 44—45 The hidden God will be revealed.

Isaiah 49 God promises that His salvation will reach to the ends of the earth. The light will reach the Gentiles in darkness. All flesh will know that the Lord is Savior and Redeemer.

Isaiah 50 Rely on God. Trust in the name of the Lord.

Isaiah 51 Look to the Lord and live in light of His eternal promises. The ransomed of the Lord will obtain gladness and joy. The Lord will comfort His people.

Isaiah 52:13—53:12 A vivid prophecy of the Messiah. It declares His suffering according to the will of God and His triumphant resurrection from the dead. By His wounds we are healed. He will see His offspring and prolong His days.

Isaiah 55 Seek the Lord while He may be found. Turn from wickedness. Find pardon in His promise. His way are not our ways, His thoughts are not our thoughts.

Isaiah 57:20—21 No peace for the wicked.

Day 57

Read Isaiah 58—Jeremiah 3

Form Check

Isaiah 58 God was not moved by their partial adherence to the covenant.

Isaiah 59:2 Sin causes a separation from God.

Isaiah 60:15–22 Then you will know that the Lord is Savior and Redeemer.

Isaiah 61:1–3 Jesus quotes from this passage to declare His purpose on earth.

Isaiah 62:6–7 Take no rest and give God none until His promises are fulfilled. This is an example of faithfulness in prayer.

Isaiah 64:8 God is a loving father and potter. We are the work of His hand.

Isaiah 66:2 The Lord looks to one who is humble, contrite, and trembles at His word.

Jeremiah 1:1–3 Jeremiah prophesied from Josiah's reign until the exile of Jerusalem. Review 2 Kings 22—25 and 2 Chronicles 34—36 for context.

Jeremiah 1—3 Jeremiah is called to proclaim Judah's unfaithfulness to the Lord.

Cool Down

Isaiah

Major Theological Themes

1. God's Sovereignty

2. God's Coming Righteous Judgment

3. Salvation by Grace through Faith

4. The Remnant

5. The Coming Messiah and His Righteous Rule

Day 58

Read Jeremiah 4–15

Form Check

Jeremiah 5 Humbly seek the Lord. Don't be ignorant of His ways. Don't refuse correction.

Jeremiah 7:1–11 Preaching repentance to those who are practicing idolatry while thinking they are worshipping the Lord. Remember the Golden Calf.

Jeremiah 7:23–24 God commanded His people to walk in His ways but they turned away from Him. They walked in their own ways.

Jeremiah 8:3 Remember Deuteronomy 30:15–20.

Jeremiah 9:1–6 Through deceit they refuse to know the Lord.

Jeremiah 9:23–24 Boast in nothing other than knowing the Lord.

Jeremiah 10 Trusting in idols is foolish.

Jeremiah 11:1–17 All of God's words are true. His promises and His warnings. He is faithful to do all He has said.

Jeremiah 14:7–12 Their cries of repentance and for God to act for His name's sake are superficial. God says He won't listen because they have loved to wander and have not kept their feet in check.

111

Day 59

Read Jeremiah 16–29

Form Check

Jeremiah 17:9–10 The heart is deceitful. Don't follow it. Remember Numbers 15:37–41.

Jeremiah 18 God is sovereign. He is the potter. He molds the clay however He sees fit.

Jeremiah 20:7–18 Jeremiah's ministry was hard. People love the false prophets, not the true.

Jeremiah 22:15–16 This is what it means to know the Lord. Natural fruits of a heart right with God.

Jeremiah 23:5–6 God's righteous Messiah is coming from the lineage of David.

Jeremiah 24:7 God promises them a new heart.

Jeremiah 25 God lovingly sent prophets. The people refused to listen. The people who survive will be exiled seventy years.

Jeremiah 25:15 The imagery of the cup of God's wrath will be important in the New Testament.

Jeremiah 26:1–6 Life and death are set before them.

Jeremiah 29 Jeremiah encourages the exiles to be faithful to God. To heed God's promises and commands, not the words of the false prophets.

Day 60

Read Jeremiah 30-43

Form Check

Jeremiah 30:21 People foolishly think they can approach God however they want. It's dangerous.

Jeremiah 31:27–40 A New Covenant is promised.

Jeremiah 32:16–22 Jeremiah's prayer appeals to God's character and ways. Compare Exodus 33:13.

Jeremiah 33 Restoration and the coming Davidic kingdom are promised.

Jeremiah 35:12–16 The Lord is more worthy of being obeyed than any other authority.

Jeremiah 36:24 Jehoiakim was a wicked king. Remember 2 Kings 23:37 and 2 Chronicles 36:5–8.

Jeremiah 39:11–14 Jeremiah had been abused by his own people. Now he was cared for by enemies of his people.

Jeremiah 42:1–6; 43:1–4 The people seek a word from the Lord. They claim to be willing to obey even if it is difficult. They were not willing.

Jeremiah 42:7 Jeremiah knew the Lord would respond to him. The text says that the answer came at the end of ten *days*. Many people aren't willing to wait ten *seconds* to hear God's response in prayer.

Be Encouraged

More than half way! Keep going. Don't quit. Your
investment in your knowledge of God's word is well
worth it.

*98 Your commandments make me wiser than my
enemies,*
For they are ever mine.
99 I have more insight than all my teachers,
For Your testimonies are my meditation.
100 I understand more than the aged,
Because I have observed Your precepts.
101 I have restrained my feet from every evil way,
That I may keep Your word.
102 I have not turned aside from Your ordinances,
For You Yourself have taught me.
103 How sweet are Your words to my taste!
Yes, sweeter than honey to my mouth!
104 From Your precepts I get understanding;
Therefore I hate every false way.
105 Your word is a lamp to my feet
And a light to my path.

–Psalm 119:98–105

Day 61

Read Jeremiah 44–52

Form Check

Jeremiah 44:1–19 The people refuse to repent. They persist in their unfaithfulness and spiritual idolatry. They will not walk in the ways of the Lord.

Jeremiah 46:10 A day of vengeance is described.

Jeremiah 48:10 Cursed is the one who does the Lord's work negligently.

Jeremiah 49:19 No one can stand against the Lord or against His judgments.

Jeremiah 50:6 Leadership is capable of leading people astray. Leaders will be held accountable. The people, also, are tasked with being careful whom they submit themselves to.

Jeremiah 51:15–26 The Lord is powerful. Glorious. Even the most powerful nations of earth are an instrument in His hand. They can be used by Him to glorify His name.

Jeremiah 52 The fall of Jerusalem, destruction of the temple, and exile of the people are recorded.

Day 62

Read Lamentations 1—Ezekiel 11

Form Check

How does Lamentations relate to God's promises and warnings? Compare to Deuteronomy 28.

Lamentations 3:22–23 Great is God's faithfulness.

Lamentations 4:12 No one imagined it would be possible for Jerusalem to fall.

Ezekiel 1 A truly awesome vision of the glory of God.

Ezekiel 2:1 The phrase "son of man" is first used in Ezekiel. It will appear 92 more times in Ezekiel.

Ezekiel 3 Ezekiel is told people will not listen, even though they should. Ezekiel is not responsible for their response. He must be faithful to proclaim.

Ezekiel 5:5–17 God's judgment is upon Israel. They failed to walk with God in His commandments.

Ezekiel 6:9 God's feelings toward apostasy.

Ezekiel 8:4 Ezekiel sees the glory of God again.

Ezekiel 8 God's response to idolatry.

Ezekiel 10 The glory of God departs.

Ezekiel 11:18–21 Ezekiel declares God's promise to give a new heart to His people to walk with Him.

Cool Down

Jeremiah & Lamentations

Major Theological Themes

1. Judgment
2. Apostasy
3. Repentance
4. God's Wrath
5. The New Covenant
6. God's Faithfulness and Mercy

Day 63

Read Ezekiel 12-24

Form Check

Ezekiel 13 False prophets strongly denounced.

Ezekiel 14:1–8 Idolatry in the heart.

Ezekiel 15:8 Judgment because the people acted unfaithfully.

Ezekiel 16 Harlotry and adultery. Vivid terms for the people's unfaithfulness and violation of the covenant.

Ezekiel 18:5–9 God describes the characteristics of a righteous man.

Ezekiel 18:23, 32 God does not delight in the destruction of the wicked.

Ezekiel 20:18–26 God commanded His people to walk in His ways. They turned away from Him. God acts for the glory of His name.

Ezekiel 21:27 A messianic prophecy.

Ezekiel 23 Judah's unfaithfulness is worse than Israel's.

Ezekiel 24:15–27 God is sovereign. Many are willing to follow the Lord when He blesses them. Are you willing to follow in circumstances like Ezekiel experienced? God is worthy in all circumstances.

Day 64

Read Ezekiel 25-38

Form Check

Ezekiel 28:1–19 Explicitly about the king of Tyre. Like Isaiah 14's description of the king of Babylon, it seemingly goes beyond to describe Satan as well.

Ezekiel 30:20–26 God is sovereign over the nations.

Ezekiel 33:1–20 The watchman must warn. How people respond to the warning is not the responsibility of the watchman.

Ezekiel 33:30–33 People come to Ezekiel, enjoy hearing the word of God, but aren't practicing God's ways. Judgment is still upon them. Compare Jesus' statements in Luke 6:46 and Matthew 7:24–27.

Ezekiel 34:1–10 Judgment upon the false, foolish, and wicked shepherds. Contrary to this description, Jesus is the Good Shepherd (John 10:11–16).

Ezekiel 34:23–24 Fulfilled in Jesus of Nazareth, the Christ.

Ezekiel 35 God promises to judge Edom completely.

Ezekiel 36:22–32 A new heart is promised. Not for their sake. For the sake of God's great name.

Ezekiel 37:11–14 God explains the vision.

Day 65

Read Ezekiel 39-48

Form Check

Ezekiel 39:7–8 God will act for the sake of His holy name.

Ezekiel 40—48 The description of the temple may not strike modern readers with the same significance it had for Ezekiel. Remember,

- Ezekiel saw the vision of the glory of God depart from the temple because of the idolatry of the people; and
- Ezekiel prophesied about the judgment coming upon Jerusalem and the destruction of the temple.

With these terrible visions in mind, Ezekiel was blessed to see God promise to restore His promises for the sake of His great name. The lengthy description in these chapters would have been a great encouragement to Ezekiel and his original readers/hearers.

Ezekiel 43:1–5 Vision of the glory of God returning to fill the house of God again.

Ezekiel 47:13–23 The inheritance is restored.

Ezekiel 48:35 The presence of the Lord among His people is an exclamation point to end this prophecy.

Cool Down

Ezekiel

Major Theological Themes

1. God's Sovereignty
2. God's Judgment
3. God's Glory and Presence Among His People

What is the Babylonian Exile? This terminology often refers to the destruction of Jerusalem in 586 BC by Babylon and the exile that followed. However, there were two exiles before this at the hands of the Babylonians. The first occurred during the reign of Jehoiakim (605 BC) and the second during the reign of Jehoiachin (597 BC). Ezekiel came to Babylon during the exile under Jehoiachin. See Ezekiel 1:1–3, 2 Kings 24:8–16, and 2 Chronicles 36:9–10.

Day 66

Read Daniel 1-12

Form Check

Daniel 1:8–21 Daniel resolved to remain faithful in the midst of a land of idols. God gave Daniel and his friends abundant favor.

Daniel 2:17–28 Daniel prays for God's compassion. He is careful to give all glory and honor to God.

Daniel 3:18 Death is preferable to idolatry for Shadrach, Meshach and Abed-nego.

Daniel 4:34–37 Nebuchadnezzar, king of Babylon, is humbled and gives glory to God.

Daniel 5:17–24 God is sovereign. He brings judgment on nations that refuse to glorify Him.

Daniel 6:25–28 King Darius honors the Lord.

Daniel 7:9–14 The Son of Man is presented before the Ancient of Days. Compare to Isaiah 42:8, 48:11. Jesus is the Son of Man described here.

Daniel 8:16, 9:21 Gabriel is one of two angels named in Scripture. The other is Michael.

Daniel 9:1–2 Daniel reads Jeremiah.

Daniel 9:7–14 Daniel laments in prayer for the failure of his people to walk in the ways of the Lord.

Daniel affirms that God was righteous to pour out judgments for the sake of His name.

Daniel 9:20–27 A messianic prophecy.

Daniel 10:10–21 The messenger was dispatched as soon as Daniel began praying, but he was withstood twenty-one days. The archangel Michael is referenced as helping overcome the spiritual warfare.

Daniel 12:3 These words are for the end of time.

Cool Down

Daniel

Major Theological Themes

1. God's Faithfulness

2. Prayer

3. The Coming Kingdom of The Son of Man

4. The Sovereignty of God

5. The Pride of Humanity

6. The End Times

What is the Babylonian Exile? The first deportation and exile happened during the reign of Jehoiakim in 605 BC. Daniel went to Babylon during this first exile. The second exile and deportation happened during the reign of Jehoiachin in 597 BC. The third deportation happened in 586 BC when Jerusalem fell and the temple was destroyed. See 2 Kings 23:34—24:7, 2 Chronicles 36:5–8, and Daniel 1:1–7.

Warm Up: The Minor Prophetic Books (Pre-Exilic)

Hosea, Joel, Amos, Obadiah, Jonah, Micah, Nahum, Habakkuk, & Zephaniah

The remaining prophetic books are the Minor Prophets. These twelve books can also be grouped into two broad categories:

- Pre-Exilic
- Post-Exilic

The Pre-Exilic prophets prophesied and wrote prior to the destruction of Jerusalem by the Babylonians.

These books follow the Major Prophets in the canon. That doesn't mean they follow chronologically. They should be overlaid with the Major Prophets on the timeline recorded in Samuel, Kings, and Chronicles.

Some view the message of the prophets as harsh. Quite the contrary! The prophets of God lovingly sound the call to repentance and redemption. The God of justice could bring judgment *without* sending prophets. Instead, He sends enforcers of the covenant to call His people back to Him. God is longsuffering, patient, merciful, and kind. The prophets are proof.

Day 67

Read Hosea 1—Joel 3

Form Check

Hosea 1:1 Hosea ministered in the same period as Isaiah. Hosea preached to the northern kingdom of Israel. Compare Isaiah 1:1, 2 Kings 15—20, and 2 Chronicles 26—32.

Hosea 1:2 The imagery of spiritual harlotry and unfaithfulness speak of Israel forsaking God.

Hosea 1:9 Compare to Exodus 19:5–6. They have violated the covenant.

Hosea 4 God rebukes the people of Israel because they have forsaken Him in their unfaithfulness.

Hosea 6:1–3 Press on to know the Lord.

Hosea 6:6 Quoted twice by Jesus in Matthew's Gospel.

Joel 1:15 The phrase "the day of the Lord" appears for the first of five times in this short book.

Joel 2:13 Return to the Lord. He is gracious.

Joel 2:28–31 Promise of the Holy Spirit. Quoted in Acts 2.

Joel 2:32 Whoever calls on the name of the Lord will be saved. Quoted in Acts 2:21 and Romans 10:13.

Cool Down

Hosea

Major Theological Themes

1. Repentance
2. Spiritual Adultery
3. God's Covenantal Faithfulness and Love
4. God's Wrath Toward Sin

Who is Ephraim in Hosea? Ephraim was the largest tribe of the northern kingdom of Israel. In this prophecy, Ephraim is used to refer to the entire northern kingdom. They have ceased striving with God. Remember where the name Israel originated; see Genesis 32:28.

***

Joel

Major Theological Themes

1. The Day of the Lord
2. God's Sovereignty
3. Salvation and Judgment

Day 68

Read Amos 1—Jonah 4

Form Check

Amos 1:1 The date of Amos' prophesying to the northern kingdom of Israel is very specific. Amos was a contemporary of Hosea and Isaiah.

Amos 1:1—2:5 Israel would have agreed with the judgments declared upon these nations.

Amos 2:6 The prophecy turns against Israel.

Amos 3:7 God reveals His will to His people. Remember Deuteronomy 29:29.

Amos 4 God works to bring His people back to Himself. God is willing to do more than most people acknowledge or realize.

Amos 5:4 Seek the Lord.

Amos 5:18–20 The prophet warns that the day of the Lord will not be what they are expecting.

Amos 5:21–24 God says He hates their half-hearted obedience.

Amos 9:8–12 God will preserve a remnant through judgment. God will establish the promised kingdom.

Obadiah 1:1 A prophecy against Edom. Remember Jeremiah 49:7–22; Lamentations 4:21–22; and Ezekiel 25:12–14, 35:1–15.

Obadiah 1:15 The day of the Lord is near for all nations.

Jonah 1:1 This prophecy isn't dated by the prophet. We have read about Jonah already in 2 Kings 14:25.

Jonah 1:4, 17; 2:10; 4:6–8 God is sovereign over all of creation, including creatures both large and small. Only the prophet disobeys the Lord in this account.

Jonah 3:10 A helpful passage for understanding true repentance. A change of mind is followed by a true change of deeds. God saw their deeds.

Jonah 4:1–2 Jonah didn't want God to save the wicked enemies of Israel. Jonah complains that the God is too gracious, compassionate, merciful, and kind. This is contrary to how many modern people think of the God of the Old Testament. Jesus reveals the Father. The God of the New Testament and the Old Testament is the same.

Cool Down

Amos

Major Theological Themes

1. Social Justice
2. Religious Hypocrisy
3. The Day of the Lord

***

Obadiah

Major Theological Themes

1. Judgment and Salvation
2. God's Sovereignty over the Nations

***

Jonah

Major Theological Themes

1. Divine Sovereignty and Human Will
2. God's Mercy and Kindness

Day 69

Read Micah 1—Zephaniah 3

Form Check

Micah 1:1 Micah was a contemporary of Isaiah, Amos, and Hosea.

Micah 3:12 Quoted in Jeremiah 26:18.

Micah 4:1–5 The nations will stream to the Lord and will walk in His ways. Remember Isaiah 2:2–4.

Micah 5:2–5 A prophecy of the Messiah which covers both His first and second advents.

Micah 6:8 God told us what is good: to act justly, to love kindness, and to walk humbly with God.

Micah 7 Wait for the Lord. He alone is the hope of His people. God delights in unchanging love.

Nahum 1:1 Nahum preaches a message of condemnation upon Nineveh 150–130 years after Jonah. This is the message Jonah would have preferred to preach.

Nahum 1:2–8 The character, power, and glory of God are vividly declared. The Lord is good. He knows those who take refuge in Him.

Habakkuk 1:13 God is too pure to look upon evil with favor.

Habakkuk 2:4 The righteous will live by faith. Quoted in Romans 1:17; Galatians 3:11; and Hebrews 10:38.

Habakkuk 2:14 The knowledge of the glory of the Lord will fill the earth.

Habakkuk 2:20 Be silent before the Lord.

Zephaniah 1:1 Zephaniah was the great-great-grandson of King Hezekiah. He prophesied during the days of Josiah. See 2 Kings 22—23 and 2 Chronicles 34—35.

Zephaniah 1:14–18 The day of the Lord is near. It is a day of wrath. Remember Proverbs 11:4.

Zephaniah 3:9–10 God will purify and gather His worshippers to Himself.

Cool Down

Micah

Major Theological Themes

1. God's Covenantal Faithfulness
2. The Coming Messiah
3. Social Justice

***

Nahum

Major Theological Theme

1. God's Sovereignty over the Nations

***

Habakkuk

Major Theological Themes

1. God's Sovereignty over the Nations

2. God's Mercy and Justice

3. God's Righteousness

***

Zephaniah

Major Theological Themes

1. Judgment and Salvation

2. The Dangers of Idolatry and Religious Hypocrisy

3. The Day of the Lord

4. God's Sovereignty over the Nations

Warm Up: Minor Prophets (Post-Exilic)
Haggai, Zechariah, & Malachi

Jerusalem was destroyed by Babylon in 586 BC. The survivors were exiled. This was God's judgment for the sins of Manasseh and the refusal of His people to heed the word of the prophets (2 Kings 24:2–4; 2 Chronicles 36:15–21).

The Babylonians were defeated by the Persians in 539 BC. Cyrus issued a decree that all Jews could return to Jerusalem to re-build the temple (Ezra 1:1–3; 2 Chronicles 36:22–23).

Fifty thousand exiles returned. The rebuilding process began but was halted because of opposition (Ezra 2:64–65; 4:1–5).

Haggai and Zechariah began their prophetic ministry during this period. This was before Ezra and Nehemiah came to Jerusalem (c. 520—480 BC).

The historical books of Ezra and Nehemiah recount the first return of the Jewish people (538 BC) through the efforts of Ezra and Nehemiah. Ezra led a second return to Judah in c. 458 BC.

Malachi is the final writing prophet in the Old Testament. His ministry began less than a century after the temple was completed. Spiritual apathy and unfaithfulness had already begun to take root again.

Day 70

Read Haggai 1—Zechariah 8

Form Check

Haggai 1:1 No longer dating by kings of Israel and Judah. Second year of Darius, sixth month, first day.

Haggai 1:12–13 The people obeyed the voice of the Lord. The Lord promised He was with them.

Haggai 2:9 God promises that the glory of the second temple will be greater than the first. The second temple was less impressive to look at. Yet, the second temple is the one the Messiah came to.

Haggai 2:10 Second year, ninth month, twenty-fourth day.

Haggai 2:11–14 The state of being unclean can spread and defile that which was formerly clean. Sin infects and defiles. Remember Isaiah 6:5; 64:6.

Haggai 2:20 Second time, same day as 2:10.

Zechariah 1:1 Second year of Darius, eighth month.

Zechariah 2:11 Many nations will join themselves to the Lord and be His people.

Zechariah 3:8–10; 6:11–15 A messianic prophecy.

Zechariah 4:6 Not by might or power, but by the Spirit of the Lord.

Zechariah 7:4–7 God isn't fooled by going through the motions. Remember Isaiah 58.

Zechariah 7:8–14 They refused to pay attention. They made their hearts hard so they couldn't hear the law. Therefore, great wrath came from God against them.

Zechariah 8:14–17 The Lord acts with purpose, both to do harm and to do good.

Cool Down

Haggai

Major Theological Themes

1. The Great Commandment
2. Avoid Spiritual Apathy
3. God's Abiding Presence with His People
4. Holiness is Not Transmitted by Contact
5. God is Sovereign and Faithful

Day 71
Read Zechariah 9—Malachi 4

Form Check

Zechariah 9:9 The Messianic king enters Jerusalem.

Zechariah 11:12–13 The Messiah is rejected.

Zechariah 12:10 They will mourn over the death of the Messiah.

Zechariah 13:7 Fulfilled in Matthew 26:31 and Mark 14:27.

Zechariah 14:1–15 The Messiah will return in glory.

Malachi 1:2–3 God speaks of His love in terms of His covenantal faithfulness to the nation.

Malachi 1:4–5 God fulfilled His promise to judge Edom. Remember, for example, Ezekiel 35.

Malachi 1:10–12 God's name will be great among the nations. Yet, His people are profaning it.

Malachi 2:17 Their words are wearying to the Lord.

Malachi 3:1 A prophesy fulfilled by John the Baptist and Christ. The Lord will come to His temple.

Malachi 3:6 Remember Malachi 1:2–5.

Malachi 4:1–6 Behold, the day is coming.

Cool Down

Zechariah

Major Theological Themes

1. Spiritual Apathy
2. Salvation of the Nations
3. The Coming Messiah

Malachi

Major Theological Themes

1. God's Sovereignty
2. Election
3. God is Faithful
4. The Coming Judgment

Warm Up: The Gospels & Acts

Matthew, Mark, Luke, John & Acts

After the close of the Old Testament canon, God was silent for roughly four centuries. No prophets. No new inspired writings.

During this silent period, the people of God have largely returned from exile. They reinstituted temple worship. This began because of permission from the Persian Empire. When the New Testament period begins much of the context is similar. However, the major governmental power has changed. Twice.

From the Persians to the Greeks, then to the Greco-Roman Empire.

The Gospels and Acts record historical narrative of the advent of the Messiah and the beginnings of His church. God's silence was over.

In this Bible program, we're going to keep Luke & Acts together. They were written by the same author.

Matthew, Mark, and Luke are referred to as synoptic Gospels because they share so much content. John's Gospel is unique. It contains much that is not found in the others. Some feel a need to reconcile the Gospels. Resist this urge. Instead, see each Gospel as inspired and providing its own perspective.

The differences in perspective are important. It's why we have four Gospels instead of one.

Day 72

Read Matthew 1–14

Form Check

Matthew 1:1–17 Matthew provides insight into the perspective of his Gospel with this genealogy. He is interested in showing that Christ is the Messiah, the Son of David. Remember 2 Samuel 7:8–17.

Matthew 1:22–23 Matthew uses this approach more than any other Gospel writer. Showing fulfillment of Old Testament prophecies in the events he records.

Matthew 3:1–12 Remember Isaiah 40:3 and Malachi 3:1; 4:5–6. John is preparing the way by declaring the need for repentance and bearing fruit.

Matthew 4:1–11 Satan attempts to get Jesus to test the Lord instead of trusting the Lord. Satan does so by quoting Scripture.

Matthew 7:21–23 Remember Amos 5:18–20. "Many" is a scary word.

Matthew 8:3 Jesus touched the unclean. Instead of Jesus becoming unclean, He cleansed the leper. Remember Leviticus and Haggai 2:10–14.

Matthew 8:14–17 This fulfilled Isaiah 53:4. How many times does this passage need to be fulfilled?

Matthew 9:9 Jesus calls Matthew, the author of this Gospel. He was a tax-collector, not a fisherman.

Matthew 9:36–38 Jesus instructs the disciples to pray for laborers.

Matthew 10 Jesus sends them out after instructing them. In partial fulfillment of the prayer in 9:36–38.

Matthew 11:2–6 Jesus quotes from prophecies in Isaiah that John knew well. Jesus intentionally leaves out part of Isaiah 61:1. The part Jesus left out is most applicable to John's circumstances. Blessed is the one who does not take offense at Christ.

Matthew 11:25–30 Jesus praises the Father. Both for hiding and for revealing these things.

Matthew 12:46–50 Jesus' family are the ones who do the will of the Father in heaven.

Matthew 13:18–23 The "many" from Matthew 7 likely come from the rocky and thorny soils. Pay attention. Don't be deceived.

Matthew 14:13–14 While grieving the death of John the Baptist, Jesus still has compassion on others.

Matthew 14:22–33 Peter is often criticized for his failing faith. Remember, the rest of them never even got out of the boat!

Day 73

Read Matthew 15–28

Form Check

Matthew 15:3 Don't transgress the word of God because of the traditions of men.

Matthew 15:15–20 Remember Numbers 15:37–41 and Jeremiah 17:9.

Matthew 16:13–20 The Father revealed Christ's true identity to Peter. Based on this true confession — that Jesus is the Son of God — Jesus promised to build His church. The gates of Hades won't be able to withstand the advance of Christ's church.

Matthew 16:24–27 Jesus says this is true for anyone who wants to follow Him. Not just some.

Matthew 17:22–23 Jesus knows His mission.

Matthew 18:35 Unforgiveness is dangerous.

Matthew 19:12 Jesus acknowledges this is a hard teaching. If you can accept it, you should.

Matthew 20:17–19 Jesus tells them plainly. Again.

Matthew 21:1–11 Remember Zechariah 9—11. This initial acceptance was prophesied to turn hostile.

Matthew 21:12–13 Jesus demonstrates holy anger. Anger itself isn't a sin. Jesus never sinned.

Matthew 22:1–14 Many are called. Few are chosen.

Matthew 22:31–32 Jesus refutes their doctrine with grammar. Pay careful attention to what you are reading. The details are important. Don't rely on systems but on every word of God.

Matthew 23:37 Jesus longs to gather them but *they* are unwilling.

Matthew 24:42 Be ready. Stay alert.

Matthew 26:13 This simple act will be remembered and spoken of in the whole world.

Matthew 26:54 It must all be fulfilled perfectly.

Matthew 27:45 It wasn't the wrath of the Jews or the Romans that made the land go dark. It was the wrath of God.

Matthew 28:18–20 All authority in heaven and earth have been given to Christ. This isn't a suggestion. It is a command. It is accompanied by a beautiful promise of Christ's abiding presence until the end.

Cool Down

Matthew

Major Theological Themes

1. Jesus is the Messiah, the Son of David
2. Discipleship
3. The Kingdom of Heaven
4. The Great Commission

Day 74

Read Mark 1–16

Form Check

Mark 1:1 The beginning of the gospel.

Mark 1:14–15 Jesus preached the gospel. The kingdom of God is at hand. Repent and believe.

Mark 3:20–30 People thought Jesus was out of His mind. They credited the Holy Spirit's work to Satan.

Mark 4:24 Take care what you listen to.

Mark 5:18–20 Jesus sent this man away to proclaim God's great deeds and mercy.

Mark 6:5–6 Unbelief is powerful.

Mark 6:12 They were sent out and began preaching the same gospel Jesus preached.

Mark 7:8–9 Don't become an expert at setting aside God's commandments for the traditions of men.

Mark 7:14–23 Evil flows from within. It defiles. This is why salvation could never be by our works.

Mark 8:34–38 Jesus teaches about the meaning of belief and following Him.

Mark 9:19 Jesus is irritated by unbelief.

Mark 10:18 No one is good except God alone.

Mark 10:45 The Son of Man came to serve and to give His life as a ransom for many.

Mark 12:28–31 The greatest commandments (Deuteronomy 6:4–5; Leviticus 19:18). Violating these are, therefore, the greatest sins.

Mark 13:10 The gospel must be preached to all nations.

Mark 13:37 Jesus says to all: "Be on the alert!"

Mark 14:62 Jesus declares His identity as the Son of Man prophesied in Daniel 7:13–14.

Mark 15:34 Jesus quotes the first line of Psalm 22. Jesus is teaching even during His suffering in fulfillment of Scripture.

Mark 16:9–20 There is a lot of controversy and debate over the ending of Mark's Gospel. This controversy does not need to cause stumbling or confusion. It is most likely that the original Gospel ended at 16:8. Material was likely added at a later time which then became part of the canonical writing. If the longer ending was not original to Mark, it would not be the first time a book of Scripture had material added at the end. See Deuteronomy 34 and Joshua 24:29–33 for example.

Cool Down

Mark

Major Theological Themes

1. Following Jesus

2. Discipleship

3. Jesus, Suffering Servant

4. Jesus, Son of God

5. Jesus, Son of Man

6. Jesus, Savior of both Jew and Gentile

Day 75

Read John 1–12 (Skip Luke)

Form Check

John 1:1 John's Gospel begins with a declaration of the divinity of the Word and an identification of two Persons that are God. The Apostle John had a trinitarian understanding of the true and living God.

John 1:12–13 As many as received Him received the right to become children of God.

John 1:14 The Word became flesh. Jesus of Nazareth is the Word of God.

John 2:13–22 After making a whip and driving people out of the temple the people ask for a sign. Jesus declares His resurrection will be the sign.

John 3:3 Unless a person is born again, they cannot see the kingdom of God.

John 3:14–15 Remember Numbers 21:6–9.

John 3:36 A good memory verse.

John 4:24 God is spirit. Those who worship Him must worship in spirit and truth.

John 4:34 Jesus' food is to do the will of the Father and to accomplish His work.

John 5:24 The one who believes has passed from death into life.

John 5:39–47 Moses wrote about Jesus. Eternal life isn't in the Bible, it's in Christ. The Bible testifies about Jesus.

John 6:28–29 Notice the contrast between works (plural) and the work (singular) of God.

John 6:41–58 In context, Jesus isn't talking about communion. This isn't the Last Supper. No one eats any bread. No one drinks any wine. None are offered. Jesus is talking about something else.

John 6:66–69 Many turned away from Jesus after walking with Him for a little while.

John 7:37–39 Jesus speaks of the Holy Spirit. Remember Isaiah 55.

John 8:31 If you continue in Christ's word, then you are a genuine disciple of Jesus. If.

John 8:58–59 They clearly understood Jesus' claim to be God. They attempted to put Him to death for blasphemy because they did not believe.

John 9:38 Jesus receives worship and does not correct the man.

John 10:11 Jesus is the Good Shepherd. Remember Ezekiel 34:12; 34:23–24; 37:24 and Isaiah 40:10–11.

John 12:32 Jesus was lifted up (crucified) to draw all men to Himself.

Day 76

Read John 13–21

Form Check

John 13:1–30 Jesus washed their feet, including Judas, knowing he was about to betray Him.

John 13:35 People will know Christ's disciples by this: their love for one another.

John 14:6 Jesus is the way, the truth, and the life. He is the only way to come to the Father.

John 14:15–24 Love and obedience go together. Verse 21 is one of the most wonderful promises in all of Scripture.

John 15:1–11 Verse 10 explains how to abide in Christ and bear much fruit to the glory of the Father.

John 15:14 Are you a friend of Jesus? Don't answer based on your feelings but based on Jesus' words.

John 15:18–19 Jesus said the world hates Him and will hate those who follow Him out of the world, too.

John 16:7 It is advantageous for Christ to go away so the Helper (Holy Spirit) will come.

John 17:3 This is eternal life. Compare this definition to the promise of John 14:21.

John 17:20–21 Jesus prays for all believers. He prays we would all be one, so that the world will believe that the Father sent Him.

John 18:5–6 When Jesus declares His identity, it is also a declaration of His divinity. Compare Exodus 3:14 and John 8:58–59. Even His unbelieving pursuers draw back and fall to the ground at this.

John 19:7 The Jews understood Christ's claims. They rejected Him and His claim in unbelief.

John 19:15 They reject their King.

John 19:36–37 This was to fulfill the Scriptures.

John 20:22 Jesus breathed on them and told them to receive the Holy Spirit.

John 20:30–31 John explains the purpose for writing this Gospel.

John 21 Many commentators view this as an Appendix. However, it is best to view this as continuing John's message: "Come to Jesus. Believe in Him. Follow Him wherever and however He leads." The modern message often stops short by saying only, "Come and believe." True, saving belief will result in following Christ until the end. Remember John 14:15–24; 15:1–11.

Cool Down

John

Major Theological Themes

1. Jesus, Son of God
2. Jesus, Lamb of God
3. Jesus, God Incarnate
4. Come, Believe, Follow
5. The Holy Spirit
6. New Birth

Day 77

Read Luke 1–13

Form Check

Luke 1:1–4 Luke explains his purpose for writing.

Luke 1:6 John the Baptist's parents were righteous in God's sight. They walked in all His ways.

Luke 1:32–33 The angel declares the glory of Christ.

Luke 2:24 Remember Leviticus 12.

Luke 2:34–35 Simeon declares Jesus will be opposed. Opposition will reveal the hearts of many.

Luke 2:40, 52 Compare 1 Samuel 2:26.

Luke 3:23–38 Jesus' lineage is traced back to Adam. Jesus' true humanity is being emphasized.

Luke 4:28–29 They quickly turned on Jesus. Compare Luke 4:22.

Luke 4:43 He came to preach the kingdom of God.

Luke 5:8–11 Peter is overcome with his own sinfulness when he recognizes who Jesus really is. They left everything to follow Him.

Luke 5:20–26 Forgiveness of sins is every person's greatest need. Jesus has the authority to forgive sin.

Luke 5:32 Jesus came to call sinners to repentance.

Luke 6:46 Remember Numbers 15:30–31.

Luke 7:29–30 Note the contrast. Some rejected God's purpose for themselves.

Luke 8:1–3 Luke includes some of the women travelling with Christ and states that there were many other women contributing to the ministry financially. "Many others" is feminine plural.

Luke 9:23 Jesus said this to all of them.

Luke 9:57–62 Many want to follow Christ as long as it's easy. Jesus tells them the true cost of following.

Luke 11:27–28 Jesus explains that true blessing is found in hearing and observing the word of God.

Luke 12:5 Jesus warns people to fear God, not men.

Luke 12:49–53 Christ's first coming was not to bring peace on earth.

Luke 13:24–30 Strive to enter the narrow gate.

Day 78

Read Luke 14–24; Acts 1–2

Form Check

Luke 14:11 Be humble.

Luke 15 There is joy in heaven over sinners who repent. Is there joy in your heart over this, too?

Luke 16:31 Jesus is foreshadowing His own resurrection. Even still, they will not believe because they have not believed Moses and the Prophets.

Luke 17:9–10 A slave is not thanked for doing their duty. We could never be saved by our works.

Luke 17:22–37 This passage is often used to teach the rapture. Look closely. Those "taken" are taken away in judgment. The ones who remain were preserved. Noah and Lot were the ones "left behind."

Luke 18:8 Jesus relates faith and prayer.

Luke 19:10 Christ came to seek and to save the lost.

Luke 23:27 Many followed as Jesus was being crucified. Women were mourning and lamenting.

Luke 23:30 Remember Hosea 10:8.

Luke 23:49–56 Luke includes the detail that women had accompanied Christ's ministry from Galilee.

Luke 24:25–27, 44–49 Jesus told them they would be witnesses of these things. He explained to them all the things concerning Himself in the Scriptures.

Acts 1:1–2 Luke's purpose for his second book.

Acts 1:3 Jesus spoke to them concerning the things of the kingdom of God.

Acts 1:8 The book of Acts will trace the fulfillment of these words of Jesus.

Acts 1:11 Remember Zechariah 14:4.

Acts 2 The Holy Spirit comes in fulfillment of Acts 1:4–8. God gathered faithful Jews from the entire Roman Empire to hear Peter's proclamation.

Acts 2:38–42 Repent and be baptized. Receive forgiveness of sins and the gift of the Holy Spirit. Devote yourself to the apostles' teaching, to fellowship, to the breaking of bread, and to prayer.

Cool Down

Luke

Major Theological Themes

1. Historicity of the Claims of Jesus
2. Jesus, Son of Man
3. Women of Faith
4. The Gospel to Jew and Gentile
5. The Genuine Humanity of Jesus

Day 79

Read Acts 3–14

Form Check

Acts 3:26 The blessing God intends is different than many people expect.

Acts 4:12 There is salvation in no other name.

Acts 4:23–31 They were encouraged by opposition because it was in fulfillment of God's word.

Acts 4:32–35 The quality and character of early church life is described.

Acts 5:1–11 The nearness of God is still a dangerous blessing in the New Covenant.

Acts 5:29–32 In obedience to Jesus' command they are witnesses along with the Holy Spirit.

Acts 5:41–42 They rejoiced and continued preaching and teaching every day that Jesus is the Christ.

Acts 6:1–7 Disunity begins amongst believers. It will get worse when Gentiles begin turning to Christ. Since the church is healthy, the problem is dealt with and the word of God continues to spread.

Acts 7:54–60 Stephen sees Christ standing at the right hand of God and prays for his murderers.

Acts 8:4 All the believers were equipped and began preaching the word as they scattered.

Acts 9:2 Paul persecuted followers of the Way; that is, believers in the Lord Jesus Christ.

Acts 9:31 Remember Acts 1:8. The church has expanded and is increasing. Believers are going on in the fear of the Lord and comfort of the Holy Spirit.

Acts 10:34–48 Peter obediently preaches directly to Gentiles. They believe and receive the Holy Spirit.

Acts 11:19–20 Believers continue to witness as they spread out from Jerusalem.

Acts 11:26 They were called Christians by outsiders. Their way of life and message was obvious to all.

Acts 12:1–3 The first Apostle is martyred: James, Son of Zebedee.

Acts 12:22–23 God puts Herod to death for failing to give Him glory. God sovereignly works in the lives of both believers and unbelievers.

Acts 13:18 God put up with them. Remember Matthew 17:17 and Mark 9:19.

Acts 14:21–23 They returned to the areas they were recently chased out of (Acts 14:2–7, 19–20) due to severe persecution. They put their lives in danger again in order to appoint elders in every place and to encourage the believers to continue in the faith.

Day 80

Read Acts 15-28

Form Check

Acts 15 Remember Acts 10. It is agreed upon by all the leaders that Jew and Gentile are both saved by the grace of God through faith in Christ alone.

Acts 16:1–3 Timothy joins Paul's ministry team.

Acts 16:10 The pronouns change from "they" to "we" because Luke joins with Paul at this point.

Acts 16:14 Lydia was a worshipper of God. The Lord opened her heart to believe Paul's message.

Acts 16:30–34 From the context of Acts so far, the exhortation to believe in Jesus includes an entire change of life and a commitment to walk in the Way.

Acts 17:7 Unbelievers clearly understood that Paul and his companions were preaching Jesus as King.

Acts 17:30–32 The command to repent is for all people, everywhere. Hearing of the resurrection caused some to sneer. Both are still true today.

Acts 18:27–28 Apollos powerfully demonstrated by the Scriptures that Jesus is the Christ.

Acts 19:9, 23 The Way is again referenced. This was how early followers of Christ thought of Christianity.

Acts 19:10 After two years, everyone living in Asia (the Roman province, not the continent) heard the word of the Lord. This proves their commitment to bearing witness faithfully and fervently.

Acts 20:28–32 Be on guard. Rely upon the grace of God. The church belongs to God, purchased with the blood of Christ.

Acts 22:22 They revolted at the idea of salvation being offered to the Gentiles.

Acts 24:14 The Way of followers of Christ was obvious enough to outsiders to be considered a sect.

Acts 24:24–25 When Paul discussed faith in Christ he spoke of righteousness, self-control, and the judgment to come. Felix became frightened by Paul's way of speaking of faith in Christ.

Acts 26:6–8 Paul says he is on trial for the hope promised to their fathers: the resurrection.

Acts 26:19–20 Paul clarifies his message to all (Jew and Gentile): repent, turn to God (believe), and perform deeds appropriate to repentance.

Acts 28:23–24 Paul testified about the kingdom of God and tried to persuade them about Jesus from Moses and the Prophets, from morning until evening. Some were persuaded. Others would not believe.

Cool Down

Acts

Major Theological Themes

1. The Historical Faith
2. The Kingdom of God
3. The Holy Spirit
4. The Growth of Christ's Church
5. The Advance of the Gospel
6. Witness
7. God's Providence and Sovereignty
8. Christianity as The Way

Warm Up: Paul's Epistles

Romans, 1 & 2 Corinthians, Galatians, Ephesians, Philippians, Colossians, 1 & 2 Thessalonians, 1 & 2 Timothy, Titus, & Philemon

The Apostle Paul's conversion is recorded in Acts 9 and he became the main figure of the second half of Acts. Paul wrote thirteen of the twenty-seven books contained in the New Testament canon.

These letters are grouped together. Nine of them are addressed to churches. The last four are addressed to individuals.

Acts provides valuable, inspired context for these letters and Paul's ministry in general. Just like it was best to read the Old Testament Prophets in light of Samuel, Kings, and Chronicles, it is best to consider Paul's epistles alongside Acts.

Paul's epistles are not ordered chronologically. Some prefer attempting to read them in their chronological order. We will stick to canonical order and read them straight through over the next six days.

Day 81

Read Romans 1–16

Form Check

Romans 1:2–4 Paul preaches the same gospel God promised beforehand in the Scriptures. Christ was declared with power to be the promised Son of God.

Romans 1:5 The obedience of faith. Love for Christ is demonstrated by obedience to His commands.

Romans 1:16–17 Paul is not ashamed of the gospel.

Romans 1:22–25 Exchanging the truth for a lie and worshipping created things is sin.

Romans 2:1–16 God's kindness leads to repentance. The unrepentant are storing up wrath for themselves on the day God judges the secrets of men.

Romans 3:19–31 This explanation of what God has done in Christ is worth extended, careful attention.

Romans 4 Salvation by grace through faith is not a New Covenant idea. It predates the Law of Moses.

Romans 5:8 God demonstrates His love in the death of His Son for sinners.

Romans 6 Freedom in Christ is not a license to sin. Consider yourselves dead to sin but alive to God in Christ Jesus. Remember Numbers 15:30–31.

Romans 7:7–13 The Law cannot save. However, it exposes sin and our need for a perfect Savior.

Romans 8 The Holy Spirit indwells those who belong to Christ and makes the Christian walk possible.

Romans 8:29 Believers are predestined to be conformed to the image of Christ. It is to this end that the grace of God is leading.

Romans 9—11 These three chapters must be considered together. They describe God's purpose in election (9:11), so that God would show mercy to all (11:32) and receive all the glory (11:36).

Romans 10:15 A quotation of Isaiah 52:7. Remember Nahum 1:15, too.

Romans 11:22 If you continue in God's kindness. Remember Romans 2:4.

Romans 12:2 Do not be conformed to this world. Renew your mind. Be transformed by the grace of God to His praise and glory.

Romans 13:1–2 Not popular today nor when it was originally written to believers in Rome.

Romans 14:23 Whatever is not from faith is sin.

Romans 15:5–7 Same mind according to Christ. One accord. One voice. Glorify God. Accept one another.

Romans 16:25–27 The true, eternal gospel of God leads to the obedience of faith in all nations.

Cool Down

Romans

Major Theological Themes

1. Salvation by Grace through Faith
2. The Gospel
3. Election
4. Justification and Propitiation
5. The Kingdom of God
6. Israel and the Church
7. The Purpose of the Law
8. The Holy Spirit
9. Freedom in Christ

Day 82

Read 1 Corinthians 1–16

Form Check

1 Corinthians 1:2 Corinth is in the region of Achaia (or Greece; Acts 20:2). Apollos was also influential in Corinth. See Acts 18:1–18; 19:1, 21–22; and 20:2–3.

1 Corinthians 1:10 Be unified in Christ.

1 Corinthians 1:12–17 This sounds very similar to our modern divisions over the teachings of men.

1 Corinthians 1:18 The gospel is foolishness to some, the power of God to others.

1 Corinthians 2:1–5 Paul determined to know nothing but Christ crucified, relying upon the Spirit.

1 Corinthians 3:1–9 Division is fleshly.

1 Corinthians 3:10–16 Build wisely.

1 Corinthians 4:1–2 Stewards must be found trustworthy in their stewardship of God's mysteries.

1 Corinthians 4:6 Do not go beyond what is written.

1 Corinthians 4:16–17 Paul taught this everywhere in every church. Remember the Way from Acts.

1 Corinthians 4:20 Not in words but in power. God's grace turns dead sinners into living saints.

1 Corinthians 5:13 To understand Paul's statement, review the reading from Day 14.

1 Corinthians 6:9–11 Do not be deceived.

1 Corinthians 6:20 Christians have been bought.

1 Corinthians 7 A counter-cultural teaching.

1 Corinthians 8:9 Christian liberty is not to be used to cause stumbling in others.

1 Corinthians 9:14 The Lord's direction.

1 Corinthians 9:23 Everything for the gospel's sake.

1 Corinthians 10 Don't worship a Golden Calf Jesus. An idol named "Jesus" is still an idol.

1 Corinthians 11:1–2 Imitate Paul as he imitates Christ.

1 Corinthians 11:27–34 Some are sick. Others have died ("sleep"). God's judgment is upon them. The nearness of God is still a dangerous blessing.

1 Corinthians 12—14 Spiritual gifts should lovingly be used orderly within the church for the purposes of edifying one another and glorifying God.

1 Corinthians 15 The gospel includes Christ's death, burial, resurrection, and exaltation where He currently sits. All according to the Scriptures.

1 Corinthians 15:55 Remember Hosea 13:14.

1 Corinthians 16:13–14 Be on the alert. Stand firm in the faith. Let all you do be done in love.

Cool Down

1 Corinthians

Major Theological Themes

1. Unity in Christ
2. The Gospel
3. Spiritual Gifts
4. The Resurrection
5. Freedom in Christ
6. Submission to God Ordained Authority
7. Holiness in the Church
8. Paul's Apostolic Calling and Authority
9. The Mission of the Church

How many letters did Paul write to the Corinthians? The most likely reconstruction requires four letters from Paul:

1. The first letter from Paul to the Corinthians is referred to in 1 Corinthians 5:9. This letter is not included in Scripture.

2. The Corinthians responded (1 Corinthians 7:1). Paul's second letter was in reply to this, which is our 1 Corinthians.

3. Paul then wrote a painful letter referred to in 2 Corinthians 2:3; 7:8. This letter has been lost.

4. A fourth letter from Paul was written, which is our 2 Corinthians.

Day 83

Read 2 Corinthians 1–13

Form Check

2 Corinthians 1:3–7 God is described as the Father of mercies and God of all comfort.

2 Corinthians 1:20–22 In Christ, all of God's promises are yes and amen. The Holy Spirit is the seal and a pledge, given to all who are in Christ.

2 Corinthians 2:10–11 Unforgiveness gives Satan an advantage over you. Be aware of his schemes.

2 Corinthians 2:14–17 The aroma of Christ is always pleasing to the Father. As we make Christ known, it is pleasant to those being saved and unpleasant to those who are perishing.

2 Corinthians 3:4–6 Our adequacy comes from God.

2 Corinthians 4:1–5 We are not to preach about ourselves. We are to preach Christ Jesus as Lord.

2 Corinthians 5:1—6:1 Every Christian is a new creation. Christians are ministers of reconciliation.

2 Corinthians 6:14–18 Light has no fellowship with darkness.

2 Corinthians 7:1 God has given us His promises in Christ. We ought to live in light of this, perfecting holiness in the fear of God.

2 Corinthians 8:1–6 They gave in their poverty, beyond their ability. Paul describes this as grace.

2 Corinthians 9:6–12 God loves a cheerful giver.

2 Corinthians 10:1–6 Paul doesn't walk according to the flesh. He tears down speculations and other lofty things raised against the knowledge of God.

2 Corinthians 11:28–29 The internal pressure is perhaps the greatest burden Paul faced.

2 Corinthians 12:9–10 Paul boasts in his weakness, because this is where Christ's strength is shown.

2 Corinthians 13:5 Examine yourself. See if you are in the faith. Is Jesus Christ in you?

Cool Down

2 Corinthians

Major Theological Themes

1. Paul's Apostolic Authority

2. Suffering for the Gospel

3. The Ministry of Reconciliation

4. A Theology of the Body and Resurrection

Day 84
Read Galatians 1—Colossians 4

Form Check

Galatians 1:3–9 Turning from the gospel is actually deserting the Father who called them by grace. Modifying the gospel leads only to condemnation.

Galatians 2:19–21 Live to God.

Galatians 3:13–14 See Deuteronomy 21:22–23.

Galatians 3:16 Singular rather than plural. Every word of God is inspired and important.

Galatians 3:24 The Law is intended to lead us to Christ, being justified by faith in Him.

Galatians 5:22–24 Walk by the Spirit.

Galatians 6:2 Fulfill the law of Christ.

Galatians 6:10 Especially to the household of faith.

Galatians 6:14–16 Walk according to this rule.

Ephesians 1:3–14 Father, Son, and Holy Spirit work to accomplish and apply salvation to those in Christ.

Ephesians 1:23 The church is Christ's body. The fullness of Him who fills all in all.

Ephesians 2:1–10 Salvation by grace through faith alone. We are saved to walk according to God's will.

Ephesians 3:14–19 Paul prays they would know the love of Christ and be filled to all the fullness of God.

Ephesians 4:1–16 The gifts Jesus gave to equip His body, until we all grow up to the fullness of Christ.

Ephesians 5:2 Walk in love.

Ephesians 6:10–17 See Isaiah 11:5, 52:7; 59:16–20.

Philippians 1:1 See Acts 16:11–40.

Philippians 1:27 Live worthy of the gospel. Stand firm in one spirit. Strive together for the faith.

Philippians 2:5–11 Compare to Isaiah 45:22–24.

Philippians 2:19–22 Timothy's proven worth and his commitment to seek the interests of Christ declared.

Philippians 3:6 Paul's zeal must be understood in light of Psalm 106:30–31 and Numbers 25:10–13.

Philippians 3:18–19 Don't be an enemy of the cross.

Colossians 1:7 Epaphras planted this church.

Colossians 1:10 Walk worthily of the Lord.

Colossians 1:13–23 The image of the invisible God.

Colossians 2:13–15 Christ is able to rescue those dead in their transgressions and give them life.

Colossians 3:2–3 Set your mind on Christ.

Colossians 4:2–4 Devote yourselves to prayer. Pray for God to open doors for the gospel of Christ.

Cool Down

Galatians

Major Theological Themes

1. Law Vs. Grace
2. Flesh Vs. Spirit
3. True Gospel Vs. Counterfeits
4. The Holy Spirit
5. Justification by Grace through Faith
6. False Teachers

Who were the recipients of Galatians? The recipients almost certainly include the southern Galatian region visited in Acts 13:14—14:23 (Pisidian Antioch, Iconium, Lystra, and Derbe). They could also include the churches established and strengthened in Acts 16:6 or even Acts 18:23.

＊＊＊

Ephesians

Major Theological Themes

1. The Church
2. Church Government
3. Spiritual Warfare
4. Love for each other in Christ
5. Prayer
6. The Glory and Purpose of Salvation
7. Living Worthy of the Gospel

***

Philippians

Major Theological Themes

1. Privileges of Citizenship in the Kingdom of God
2. Joy in Christ
3. Living Worthy of the Gospel
4. The Extreme Danger of False Teaching
5. Exalting Christ

***

Colossians

Major Theological Themes

1. The Glory and Exaltation of Christ
2. Dangers of False Teaching
3. Prayer
4. Living Worthy of the Gospel
5. Christ's Supremacy, Victory, and Power

Day 85

Read 1 Thessalonians 1—1 Timothy 6

Form Check

1 Thessalonians 1:1 Paul planted this church in Acts 17:1–10. Fierce persecution shortened his stay.

1 Thessalonians 1:9–10 Receiving the gospel is turning to the living God and waiting for the Son from heaven. Jesus rescues from the coming wrath.

1 Thessalonians 2:12 Walk worthily of God.

1 Thessalonians 4:1–8 Walk in a way that is pleasing to God. Rejecting this is rejecting God.

1 Thessalonians 4:11–12 Make it your ambition.

1 Thessalonians 5:1–11 Encourage one another and build one another up in this truth.

1 Thessalonians 5:14–22 God's will for His people is described. Don't quench the Spirit.

2 Thessalonians 1:6–12 The powerful and awesome return of Christ is described.

2 Thessalonians 2:13–17 God calls people through the gospel for this purpose.

2 Thessalonians 3:1 Pray that the word of the Lord will spread rapidly and be glorified.

2 Thessalonians 3:6–15 Paul commands these believers not to associate with and to keep away from those who do not walk according to the Way.

1 Timothy 1:5 The goal of Christian instruction.

1 Timothy 1:8–11 The Law is good when used lawfully. That is, to expose sin and lead people to be justified by faith in Christ. See Galatians 3:24.

1 Timothy 1:15–17 A trustworthy statement.

1 Timothy 2:1–6 Pray for everyone. God desires for all to be saved. There is one Mediator, Jesus, who gave Himself as a ransom for all.

1 Timothy 3:1 Another trustworthy statement.

1 Timothy 3:14–16 The church is the pillar and support of the truth. Take note of this common confession of the mystery of godliness.

1 Timothy 4:1–5 Be on your guard. Stay alert.

1 Timothy 4:6–10 Another trustworthy statement.

1 Timothy 5:18 Paul quotes both Deuteronomy 25:4 and Luke 10:7 as Scripture.

1 Timothy 6:9–12 Flee the pursuit of riches. Pursue righteousness, godliness, faith, love and perseverance instead.

1 Timothy 6:13–16 To Him be honor and everlasting dominion!

Cool Down

1 Thessalonians

Major Theological Themes

1. Perseverance in the Faith
2. The Return of Christ (Second Coming)
3. God's Faithfulness

✳✳✳

2 Thessalonians

Major Theological Themes

1. Idleness
2. The Return of Christ (Second Coming)
3. Apostasy
4. Perseverance

✳✳✳

1 Timothy

Major Theological Themes

1. Order in the Church
2. Sound Doctrine
3. The Danger of Loving Money
4. Proper Use of the Law

Day 86

Read 2 Timothy 1—Philemon 1

Form Check

2 Timothy 1:8–9 Don't be ashamed. God saves and calls with a holy calling according to His purpose.

2 Timothy 2:2 Instruction for preserving and passing on the faith. Remember Genesis 18:19.

2 Timothy 2:11–13 Another trustworthy statement.

2 Timothy 2:15 Be diligent. Handle the word accurately.

2 Timothy 3:1–5 These traits describe those holding to a form of godliness but denying the transformative power to conform them into Christ's image.

2 Timothy 3:16–17 The sufficiency of Scripture.

2 Timothy 4:10 Demas has turned away because of love for the world. He was faithful for a season (Colossians 4:14; Philemon 1:24). See Luke 8:13–14.

Titus 1:2 God cannot lie.

Titus 1:16 Remember Numbers 15:30–31; Matthew 7:16–29; Philippians 3:7–19; and 1 Corinthians 4:20.

Titus 2:11–14 A clear declaration of the divinity of Christ and the purpose of salvation.

Titus 3:1–8 Another trustworthy statement. Also, one of the clearest declarations that salvation is by grace through faith alone. Part of salvation includes producing good deeds. See Titus 2:7, 14; 3:8, 14.

Philemon 1:1–2 Archippus, one of the recipients of this letter, was also addressed in Colossians 4:17.

Philemon 1:10 Onesimus is also mentioned in Colossians 4:9.

Philemon 1:17–21 Philemon would have had the right to put Onesimus to death for his crimes. Instead, Paul says to accept him as he would the Apostle himself! This is asking for abundant grace and forgiveness to be demonstrated. Paul urged Philemon to exercise his freedom in Christ, laying down his rights and extending mercy instead.

Philemon 1:23 Epaphras was from Colossae (Colossians 4:12) and planted the church there (Colossians 1:7).

Cool Down

2 Timothy

Major Theological Themes

1. Faithfulness in Ministry and Doctrine
2. Suffering for the Gospel
3. Discipleship
4. The Necessity for Scripture
5. The Inspiration of Scripture
6. False Teachers

Titus

Major Theological Themes

1. Sound Doctrine
2. Church Leadership
3. Salvation by Grace through Faith
4. Regeneration
5. False Professions of Faith
6. Good Deeds

185

Why are elder qualifications slightly different in Titus and 1 Timothy? The church in Ephesus had been established for longer. So, Timothy was instructed not to appoint new believers (1 Timothy 3:6). Crete was a newer fellowship. Therefore, Titus likely had only new believers to choose from. Despite the minor differences, the basic characteristics remain constant.

✳✳✳

Philemon

Major Theological Themes

   1. Grace and Forgiveness

   2. Identity in Christ

   3. Freedom in Christ

Warm Up: The General Epistles

Hebrews, James, 1 & 2 Peter, 1, 2 & 3 John & Jude

This collection of eight books is referred to as the general or catholic epistles. In this case, catholic is meant to be taken literally. Catholic simply and literally means *universal*. It should not be confused with Roman Catholic, which refers to a specific denomination.

These epistles are addressed either to a very broad audience or to unnamed recipients. So, they are more general or universal in their appeal than the more specifically addressed letters of Paul.

Despite the general appeal, these epistles tend to not get as much attention as other books in Scripture. This is a shame. Each of them is included in the Bible for a reason. They deserve just as much attention and consideration as every other book.

Day 87

Read Hebrews 1—James 5

Form Check

Hebrews 1:1–2 God previously spoke to the fathers and prophets. Now, God has spoken in His Son.

Hebrews 2:1–2 Pay attention. Don't drift away.

Hebrews 3:12–15 Don't be hardened by sin. Take care that an evil, unbelieving heart isn't found in you. Encourage one another in this.

Hebrews 4:1 Let us fear. Don't come up short.

Hebrews 6:1–8 Press on to maturity. Build upon the foundational teachings. Bring forth fruit for the glory of God. Remember Numbers 15:30–31.

Hebrews 8:1 The main point.

Hebrews 9:22 There is no forgiveness without the shedding of blood. Christ's blood was shed for the forgiveness of sins.

Hebrews 10:19–25 Let us draw near, hold fast the confession, and consider how to stimulate one another to the glory of God.

Hebrews 10:26–32 Remember Numbers 15:30–31.

Hebrews 12:1–3 Don't grow weary. Don't lose heart. Fix your eyes on Christ and consider Him.

Hebrews 12:7–10 Be trained by the Lord's discipline. Those without discipline are illegitimate children.

Hebrews 12:14–17 Pursue peace and sanctification. Don't turn away from the Lord. Read Genesis 27:30–40 carefully. Esau sought for *his father* to repent (change his mind), but his father would not.

Hebrews 12:25–29 Don't refuse Him. Our God is a consuming fire.

Hebrews 13:1–5 Love one another. Live a holy life.

James 1:2–4 Consider it all joy when you face trials.

James 1:22–27 Pure and undefiled religion. Prove to be a doer of the word.

James 2:10 Salvation by works is impossible. If you keep the whole law yet stumble in one point, you're guilty of breaking it all.

James 3:1 Teachers will face stricter judgment.

James 4:4–10 Strong words about friendship with the world. Many of the Prophets spoke to idolatrous Israel and Judah this way; to those whose hearts weren't fully committed to the Lord. Don't be double-minded. Humble yourself before God.

James 4:17 Sin isn't always doing wrong. It can also be failing to do what you know is right.

James 5:19–20 It is loving to rebuke fellow believers who are straying from the Lord and from the faith.

Cool Down

Hebrews

Major Theological Themes

1. The New Covenant
2. The Superiority of Christ
3. Salvation by Grace through Faith
4. Perseverance
5. Christian Discipline
6. Holiness
7. The Immutability of Christ
8. Faith
9. The High Priestly Ministry of Christ

Who wrote Hebrews? Some assume Hebrews was written by the Apostle Paul. However, Hebrews stands clearly as the start of a new section in the canon since Paul's letters were arranged from longest to shortest. Although no author is named, Hebrews 2:3 indicates it was written by a second-generation believer: "It was first spoken through the Lord, it was confirmed to us by those who heard." The author is unknown. It was not Paul or any of the other Apostles. Beyond that is speculation. Although unnamed, the author should be considered a Prophet like other non-apostles who wrote books in the New Testament: Mark, Luke, and Jude.

***

James

Major Theological Themes

1. Faith and Works

2. Christian Living

3. True Religion

4. Prayer

5. Suffering and Perseverance

Does James contradict what Paul wrote in Ephesians about faith and works? No, it is not contradictory. Scripture is clear and unified. Salvation is by grace through faith alone. True, saving faith will necessarily produce good works. Works don't lead to faith. Faith <u>must</u> lead to works. If faith doesn't produce good works, then that faith is dead—just like a body without spirit/breath is dead.

Day 88

Read 1 Peter 1—2 Peter 3

Form Check

1 Peter 1:1 The Apostle Peter writes to areas the Apostle Paul ministered in. The most likely reason is this is shortly after Paul was martyred in Rome.

1 Peter 1:2 Peter writes that they were chosen to obey Jesus Christ. Obedience is part of salvation.

1 Peter 1:6–9 Endurance through trials is a tangible proof that your faith is genuine.

1 Peter 1:10–11 The Spirit of Christ spoke through the prophets. This theme is important to interpret some of Peter's later statements.

1 Peter 1:14–19 Prepare your minds for action. Obey the Lord. Peter quotes Leviticus to New Covenant believers.

1 Peter 2:1–3 Newborn babies are ravenous for milk. Relentless. Do you long like that for the word of God?

1 Peter 2:7–12 The purpose and calling of salvation.

1 Peter 2:21–25 Christ bore our sins so that we would live to righteousness and die to sin.

1 Peter 3:18–20 The Spirit of Christ preached through Noah. Remember 1 Peter 1:10–11.

1 Peter 4:1–3 The time past is sufficient for sinful living. Live for the will of God.

1 Peter 4:10–11 Instructions about spiritual gifts.

1 Peter 4:17–18 Judgment begins with believers.

1 Peter 5:10 Humbly wait for the God of all grace.

2 Peter 1:3 God has granted His people everything we need for life and godliness.

2 Peter 1:10–11 Be diligent. Make certain you belong to Christ. See Titus 1:16; Matthew 7:21–23.

2 Peter 1:20–21 All Scripture was written by men under the inspiration of God. See 2 Timothy 3:16–17.

2 Peter 2:1–3 False teachers will get people to follow their own lusts and impulses, in denial of the Lord.

2 Peter 2:4–16 Remember 1 Peter 1:10–11; 3:18–20.

2 Peter 2:15–16 Remember Numbers 22.

2 Peter 2:20–22 Don't go back to a life of sin.

2 Peter 3:1–2 Remember the words spoken by the prophets and Apostles.

2 Peter 3:11–12 Look for and hasten that day.

2 Peter 3:14–16 Peter says Paul's writings are Scripture.

Cool Down

1 Peter

Major Theological Themes

1. Persecution & Suffering for the Name of Christ
2. The Call to Obedience for Christians
3. The Christian Inheritance
4. The Purpose for Salvation
5. Walking in your Particular Gifts and Calling
6. Humility and Spiritual Warfare

***

2 Peter

Major Theological Themes

1. God's Promises, Power, & Glory
2. Diligence
3. False Teachers
4. The Antidote for Apostasy
5. God's Patience and Wrath

What is the antidote for apostasy? Remembering the apostolic and prophetic instruction and putting it into practice by the grace of God is the antidote to false teaching and apostasy.

How can we hasten or speed up the coming of the Day of the Lord if God is sovereign? Peter declares Christians ought to look for and hasten the coming day of judgment (2 Peter 3:12). To hasten means to speed up or cause to come faster. Scripture has demonstrated the truth that God works all things together according to the counsel of His will (e.g. Ephesians 1:9–12). If God's people obey Him, the process is faster. If they disobey, the process takes longer. The Old Testament history is filled with examples of this (e.g. entering the Promised Land, Jonah, etc.).

Warm Up: The Revelation

Revelation

Revelation can be a controversial book. Some ignore it. Some are afraid of it. Some twist and abuse it.

It doesn't have to be this way.

God gave this Revelation of Jesus Christ to be a blessing to His people. In fact, the book begins with a declaration of blessing upon the readers and hearers:

> *Blessed is he who reads and those who hear the words of the prophecy, and heed the things which are written in it; for the time is near.*
> –Revelation 1:3

This book is what is referred to as apocalyptic literature. The imagery is vivid. However, it is not meant to be confusing. Quite the contrary!

The vivid imagery is meant to convey truth in a manner that is able to be understood. The book is titled "The Revelation." This is an unveiling of truth, not a covering.

Most of the imagery is drawn from the Old Testament. Other images are defined within the book itself. Familiarity with the Old Testament foundation and a careful reading of the book on its own terms will clear up much of the confusion for most readers.

Pulling passages out of context leads to misunderstanding of any book, not just Revelation.

Day 89

Read 1 John 1—Revelation 10

Form Check

1 John 1:5–10 If we walk with the Lord, our sins are cleansed. If we think we are sinless, we make Him a liar and the truth isn't in us.

1 John 2:3–6 By this we know that we know Him.

1 John 2:9–11 How we treat fellow believers indicates whether we are in Light or darkness.

1 John 2:15–17 If anyone loves the world, then the love of the Father is not in them.

1 John 2:26 People were trying to deceive them. Pay attention. Many deceivers are in the world.

1 John 3:10 The children of God and the children of the devil are obvious by their deeds and (lack of) love.

1 John 3:23–24 Abide in Christ. Keep His commandments. This isn't legalism. It's eternal life and true grace. Remember John 15:5–10.

1 John 4:13 We know we abide in Christ if we have the indwelling Holy Spirit of God.

1 John 5:12–13 John wrote this letter so believers could know that they have eternal life. Examine yourself by these things and find assurance in them.

1 John 5:21 Guard yourself from idols.

2 John 1:6 This is love. Walk in it.

2 John 1:10–11 Don't fellowship with false teachers. If you do, you participate in their evil deeds.

3 John 1:2 Would you want someone to pray this for you? Do you pray this way for others? That your physical state would reflect your spiritual condition?

3 John 1:5–8 Financial support makes you a fellow worker with them.

3 John 1:9–10 The danger of prideful leaders who lord their authority over others.

Jude 1:3 Fight for the faith. It was given once for all.

Jude 1:4 Remember Numbers 15:30–31.

Jude 1:11 Cain (Genesis 4), Balaam (Numbers 22), and Korah (Numbers 16) serve as examples to avoid.

Jude 1:17–25 Remember the teaching and warnings from the Apostles. Rely on God's grace.

Revelation 1:2 John testified to the word of God and the (singular) testimony of Jesus Christ.

Revelation 1:4–7 To Him be glory and dominion forever. Remember Daniel 7:13–14.

Revelation 1:9 John was exiled because of the word of God and the (singular) testimony of Jesus.

Revelation 2:7, 11, 17, 26–28; 3:5, 12, 21
Promises to those who overcome. Compare
Revelation 12:11 to see how they overcame.

Revelation 2:14 Remember Numbers 22—24.

Revelation 4 Remember Isaiah 6.

Revelation 5 The previous chapter describes the
awesome praise of God. The Lamb is the object of
worship in this chapter and draws the attention.

Revelation 6:9 They were slain because of the word
of God and they held to the (singular) testimony.

Revelation 6:16–17 The wrath of the Lamb.
Remember Hosea 10:8 and Psalm 2:12.

Revelation 7:12 Amen. Amen.

Revelation 8:13 It's about to get worse. Woe, woe,
woe to those dwelling on earth.

Revelation 10:7 This is what God foretold.

Cool Down

1 John

Major Theological Themes

1. The Error & Danger of Gnosticism
2. Fellowship & Love
3. Truth Vs. Error
4. Jesus, God Incarnate
5. God is Love
6. Freedom in Christ
7. Propitiation

∗∗∗

2 John

Major Theological Themes

1. Christ's Commandment to Love
2. Walking in the Truth
3. Christian Hospitality

∗∗∗

3 John

Major Theological Themes

1. Christian Love
2. True Leadership
3. Giving
4. The Danger of Pride
5. Unity

***

Jude

Major Theological Themes

1. Warning about False Teaching/False Teachers
2. Contending for the Faith
3. Avoiding Apostasy
4. The Lordship of Christ

Why does Jude cite extra-biblical sources? Jude is not alone. Joshua and Samuel referred to the book of Jashar (alternately spelled Jasher; Joshua 10:13; 2 Samuel 1:18). The chronicles of the kings of Israel, Judah, of King David, Solomon, of Samuel, Nathan, Gad, and even Gentile nations were referenced many times (e.g. 1 Kings 11:41; 14:19, 29; 1 Chronicles 27:24; 1 Chronicles 29:29; Esther 2:23; 6:1; 10:2). Paul and Peter reference information not found in Scripture. Their source is outside the canon. Paul names the opponents of Moses in 2 Timothy 3:8. Peter gives information about Noah as a preacher in 2 Peter 2:5 not found in Genesis. Paul also cited a Gentile in Titus 1:12. Citing these materials is not an endorsement of everything else. Likewise, Jude cites the Book of Enoch without implying that Enoch should be included in the canon of Scripture.

Day 90

Read Revelation 11—Genesis 2

Form Check

Revelation 11:17–18 Give thanks to the Almighty.

Revelation 12:1 This imagery recalls Genesis 37:9–11. The Woman in this vision is the nation of Israel.

Revelation 12:5 The male child is Christ, born from Israel according to promise. This single verse summarizes the first advent, birth to ascension.

Revelation 12:11, 17 They overcame by the blood of the Lamb, the word of their testimony, and not loving their lives. The dragon opposes those who keep the commandments and hold to the (singular) testimony.

Revelation 13:8 The Lamb's book of life.

Revelation 14:6 People preach the gospel. See Acts 10, for example. God arranged for Peter to preach. Here, an angel preaches while flying in mid-heaven.

Revelation 14:19–20 The wine press of God's wrath.

Revelation 15:2–4 The scene is similar every time Heaven opens: they are singing praise to the Lord.

Revelation 16:21 Instead of turning to God for salvation, they blaspheme Him because of the hail.

Revelation 17:14 They will fight against the Lamb. The Lamb will overcome. He is King of kings.

Revelation 17:17 God is sovereign.

Revelation 19:7 Rejoice! The marriage of the Lamb has come. The bride has made herself ready.

Revelation 19:10 The (singular) testimony of Jesus is the spirit of prophecy. All who hold to this are one.

Revelation 19:11–16 Jesus treads the wine press.

Revelation 20:4–6 The first resurrection.

Revelation 20:7–10 When Satan is released after the thousand years, the final rebellion is short-lived.

Revelation 20:11–15 You don't want to be judged by your deeds. You want your name written in the Lamb's Book of Life. See Exodus 32:32–33; Psalm 69:28; Daniel 7:10; Philippians 4:3; & Revelation 3:5; 13:8; 17:8; 21:27.

Revelation 21:7–8 The one who overcomes inherits these promises. The rest are cast into the lake of fire.

Revelation 21:27 Those written in the book enter in.

Revelation 22:12 Remember 2 Corinthians 5:10.

Revelation 22:18–19 Remember Deuteronomy 4:2; 12:32; and Proverbs 30:6.

Genesis 1—2 Note the similarity to Revelation 21—22. Genesis 3—Revelation 20 shows how God redeems His good creation that rebelled against Him.

Final Cool Down

Revelation

Major Theological Themes

1. Jesus the Christ
2. The Testimony of Jesus Christ
3. The Return of Christ (Second Coming)
4. The End Times
5. The Sovereignty & Glory of God
6. The Lamb's Book of Life

Afterword

You did it! But you haven't crossed the finish line. You've really just begun.

Don't give up now. If you completed The Program you've already started again from the beginning.

Now it's time to set your own pace. Be prepared to continue making new observations and gaining more understanding and clarity as you read your Bible cover to cover over and over again.

We encourage you to check out our website (www.theexaltedchrist.com). You can also email us if you'd like to continue the conversation: info@theexaltedchrist.com.

Be diligent to present yourself approved to God as a workman who does not need to be ashamed, accurately handling the word of truth.

—2 Timothy 2:15

Index of Subjects

Made in the USA
Monee, IL
08 April 2020